# Beerappa

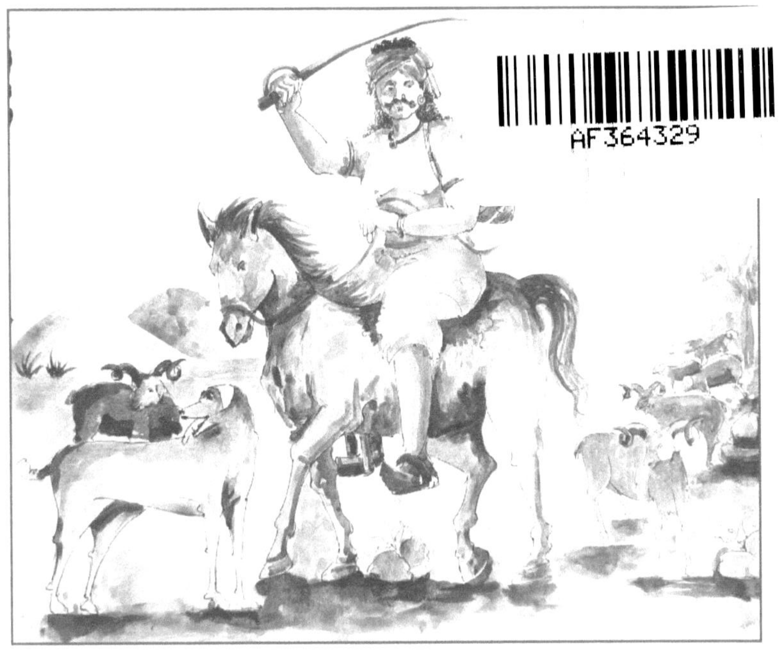

**Historical and Cultural Hero**

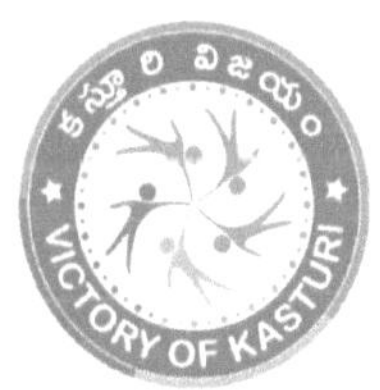



**Author**
**Dr B. Nagasheshu**

**Translated by**
**Subhash Manthri Kuruma**

# Beerappa

of
Dr B. Nagasheshu
Cell Phone: 9985509053
Email: b.nagasheshu47@gmail.com

Translated by
Subhash Manthri Kuruma
Mobile: +447799876931
Email: sbmanthri@gmail.com

Copy Right: Dr B. Nagasheshu

Published By: Kasturi Vijayam
Published on: Nov,2024

ISBN (Paperback): 978-81-974474-0-2

Print On Demand

Ph:0091-9515054998
Email: Kasturivijayam@gmail.com

Book Available
@
Amazon, flipkart

# Table of Contents

# Why I wrote

The reason I wrote this book is to make people aware of the ancient, unique, and vast culture of the indigenous shepherd (Kurubas) and the true history of the original Unsung Beerappa. Many writers are rewriting true history. I wrote this book to wake them up. As a researcher, I did not write the book using a traditional research method, but I also cannot remain silent while lies and flattery spread, as some of you may believe.

There are more than fifteen thousand pages of literature, history, and culture about the Kurubas in Kannada. Apart from stories and novels, the Kurubas themselves have a rich history of achievements. However, many Telugu people do not know the real biography of Beerappa and the Kuruba community because much of the literature is in Kannada. The Kurubas play a decisive role politically, socially, and economically in Karnataka. Hence, it was possible to compile and print fifteen thousand pages of history. Historians, writers, and researchers participated in this grand endeavor with great dedication. There are about eight volumes of literature solely on Beerappa. More than forty universities have conducted research on **Palamastula**, and over two hundred studies are being done on *Palamathas* worldwide. The prominent dynasties that ruled South India were cowherds (Kurubas), and their ruling powers were concentrated mainly in Karnataka.

In this country, the first village settlements were established by cowherds, and in this book, I refer to Kurubas as cowherds. Sheep herding is one of the oldest professions in the country. Cattle rearing began only after sheep herding, which is why Taurus comes after Aries in the zodiac signs. In fact, These tribes cannot unite due to the deceptive ideas of conversion. This has a political odor and is causing weakness. The term *"Pashu Palaku"* (animal herder) refers to Kurubas here.

The Kuruba community is a tribe that lives by herding sheep and goats in forests and hills. Kuruba is a culture, which may have developed into a caste over time. The Kurubas have a long history, which includes written records, but few people appreciate it. No one has the time or patience for it. One reason for this seems to be the delayed penetration of education into this community. Additionally, it could be said that the community is preoccupied with survival. In recent times, it is ironic that people from other castes are writing about the dynasties of cowherds as their own. To understand the Kuruba dynasties, there are many historical and legal sources available in Kannada. If anyone from other castes has doubts, they can read and understand the literature.

The reason I wrote this book is to unite the divided. If all the cowherds come together without the aspiration for political gain, the kingdom's power will belong to these cowherds. It can be said that the role of the industrial class in nation-building is critical. This country has grown so strong because of the hard work of the industrial class. Even today, we need such workers and professionals to forget caste differences and unite. We see Kuruba culture from the Neolithic period, when the people of that time built round huts on the hills to live. Around **Gunjalu pathi**, they made bamboo mats and constructed soft walls using a mixture of mud and mats, to live in these huts. Many species today were originally herders. Just as the branches of a large tree draw water from the roots, man has emerged from the forests through the roots of the cowherds. Among all the professions that contributed to civilization, animal herding is the most important. Cattle herding was the first profession in the great civilizations of the world. We must not forget the truth that all these cowherds are fruits and flowers of the same tree. I have written this book to convey this message.

The Kurubas do not fight with anyone because they herd sheep and goats, and they have to graze them on land owned by others, which has taught them from the beginning the philosophy of living without anger toward anyone. The kings who ruled India, such as the Mauryas, Satavahanas, Kadambas, Pallavas, Gangas, Badami Chalukyas, Rashtrakutas, Kalyani Chalukyas, Hoysalas, Vijayanagara kings, Seepana Yadavas, and Kakatiyas, were all rulers who provided good governance to this country, and all of them were cowherds. If anyone has doubts about the above dynasties, they can read the available books in Kannada along with the legislative sources or consult directly with historical researchers.

No matter how rich this country becomes, it cannot be a nation that does not recognize the labor of the working class. No matter how tall the buildings are, if we forget the contributions of professionals, decline is inevitable.

V

The birth story of Beerappa has been sung as a seventy-five-hour-long epic by the folk artist Siddappa Meti. No hero in the world has had their story sung for so long. If each cassette contained ninety minutes songs, sixty cassettes would be required, and these were recorded by a researcher named Veeranna Dande. It is no exaggeration to say that no hero in the world has such a vast epic. The entire story, broken into parts, amounts to a thousand pages. With fifteen stories, I had to make some changes to create a single, cohesive story without compromising its overall essence. To write the whole story would require thousands of pages. Every Indian has a caste, and each caste has a history. I had to conduct a lot of research to understand what is special about the Kuruba caste. After extensive research, this book took its current form. It took over a year of research. To write this book, I studied thirty Halumatha research texts and four books on Beerappa. I also referred to books written by renowned Kannada authors like Chandrakanta Bizzarige, Lingadalli Halappa, Siddappa Meti, and others.

Beerappa's story is a mythological tale with folk aspirations, and it appears to be a divine play of Lord Shiva. Beerappa is an aspect of Shiva. Shiva and Junjappa (another name for Sri Krishna) were revered as gods before the Europeans arrived in India. Both gods belong to the Scorpio sign. But as Europeans began to dominate, they conspired to diminish their influence. Indigenous herders (Kurubas) were forcibly converted to their religion by missionaries. Buddhism and Jainism also played a role in diminishing some of the unique practices of the **Palamatas**. Some rituals of these new religions infiltrated the customs of the **Palamatas**, leading some to mistakenly believe that these practices are their own. If religious preachers ask them to change their religion, they should demand half the wealth earned by their women as compensation. Only then will people from other religions feel ashamed.

European colonizers gave positions and power to certain individuals in India to facilitate their governance. These individuals—Reddy's, Chaudhury's, Patels, Deshmukh's, Karanam's, Patwaris, Goud's, and others—are still considered high castes. Many of today's perceptions about these groups were shaped by the circumstances of that time. Even today, these ruling elites have grown stronger and are trying to preserve that power. Wealth alone isn't enough to maintain this influence; even without wealth, some elites work to make themselves seem important. This is puzzling in today's society, where other castes witness this and harbor resentment. Some of the oppressed have even started following these rulers like slaves. Elders say that it's natural for flies to go where there is honey, but will you always live as flies? Will your offspring live like that? You must recognize when you have the potential to become an elephant. If any caste sits and criticizes, nothing will come of it. Therefore, the indigenous (Kuruba) castes and other oppressed groups must first correct their own situation.

A man's social status can only be raised through education. All oppressed castes should first focus on how to pursue education and secure their future. Education should be viewed not just as a means to a job but as a path to knowledge. These castes should not limit themselves to traditional fields but should explore new areas where they can excel and earn more. After achieving that, they can take steps toward political power. To attain political power, all oppressed groups must achieve unity. Proclaiming that one's caste is superior won't achieve anything. If we continue to fight among ourselves, counting who is more or less, minorities will use our ignorance to their advantage and take control of power.

What backward castes need is a broader mindset that includes our neighbors. Until then, power cannot be seized. In any backward caste, the members who have risen politically and economically should reach out and support others in their caste. We should help them not only in politics but in other fields as well.

Any leader who politicizes everything will remain a politician and will never be a leader in the hearts of the people. If you work to pull down those who rise, you will fall behind, and there is a danger of losing the nation. The land taken by the ruling castes indicates that the survival of other castes in this country is endangered. We can regain power at any time, but we can never reclaim the land seized by the ruling castes. My job is to create an idea. It's up to you to decide whether to implement it or not. Decide for yourselves whether you want to live as slaves or live with responsibility. The Kuruba community is unique. One of their great cultural achievements is their honor dance, and their second masterpiece is the **Kambali** (Gongali), a traditional garment registered under the name of the Kuruba caste. Their musical instruments and **Bandaru** are also connected to Kurubas. **Gudikatlu** is a unique festival in Kuruba culture. ***Oggu Katha*** is a unique folk-art form, particularly cherished by the Kurumas in Telangana. In South India, other castes regard Kurubas as auspicious, and in some places, they are invited to participate in auspicious events. Even today, this tradition is practiced in parts of Karnataka. There is a belief among farmers that if a herd of Kurubas comes, it's a good omen for sowing seeds. In some places, people who couldn't fulfill their vow to visit Tirupati Thimmappa would dedicate that offering to the local Kurubadasappa. Even today, Kurubas are respected by other communities.

Every caste member should know their history and specific customs. If every caste's history is included, human culture will shrink, and Hindu culture will grow into a larger collective culture. Life is too short to live only in the dust. Protect your existence, respect others' existence, and help others without jealousy, so that the unity and integrity of the country is preserved. All castes should unite with the spirit of ***Vasudhaiva Kutumbakam*** (the world is one family).

I would like to thank the famous Kannada writers Chandrakanta Bizzarige, Lingadalli Halappa, and Hallikere for their insights that helped me write this book. I express my deep gratitude to Professors K. Asha Jyoti and M. Ramanathannaidu, who guided me through universities. Special thanks to Dr. Rasani, Sadlapalli Chidamba Reddy, Bandi Narayanaswamy, and Mallela Narasimha, who provided suggestions during the writing process.

I also thank my children, Gagana and Tapan, who not only provided me with water, buttermilk, and food on time but also encouraged me to write well. My sincere thanks to Umadevi, who gave me the time and support I needed, and to Krishna Kumarigaru, who always inspires me in my writing. I am amazed by the generosity of Gangadharam, a retired principal in Hindupuram, who is always ready to help anyone in need. His contributions are beyond measure, and I extend my heartfelt thanks to him. I would also like to thank Kongonda Prithvivallabh Kuruma Alwal from Telangana, along with my Kuruma friends from Secunderabad. My thanks go to Madaram Krishna, who encouraged me throughout this endeavor, and to Mutta Sampat Kumar, who rallied support for the publication of this book. I also thank Mahender Barla.

Special thanks to Beere Gampamallaiah for drawing the beautiful cover of this book and to Krishnamraju for designing the cover and flawlessly completing the DTP work. I also thank Dr. Thota Venkataswamy.

My ultimate goal is for our future generations to move toward knowledge, to break free from ignorance, and to elevate the social status of our people (the downtrodden sections) through education. We should let go of superstitions and not blindly follow others. Not only Kurubas but all backward classes can improve their social status through education. This book was written with this agenda in mind. I hope you all enjoy it. The names and characters in the novel are fictional and are not meant to offend anyone but to facilitate the flow of the story. With love to you all.

**Nagasheshu**
Garimekalapalli
Ramagiri
Anantapur
Mobile: 9985509053
Email: b.nagasheshu47@gmail.com

# Translator's Note

It is with great pride and a deep sense of responsibility that I present this translation of **"Beerappa: A Historical and Cultural Hero**." Translating this remarkable work has been both a privilege and an enlightening journey, as it offers a profound look into the lives, culture, and traditions of the Kuruma community. This translation seeks to bring the unique narrative of Beerappa, a revered deity among the *Kurumas, Kurubas, and Kuruvas* in the Telugu states, to a wider audience, allowing readers to appreciate not only the heroism of Beerappa but also the deep-rooted spiritual and cultural heritage of these communities.

The story of Beerappa, has been passed down orally for generations among *the Kuruma, Kuruba, and Kuruva* communities of the Telugu states. These communities share a common cultural heritage, and Beerappa is worshipped as their caste deity in every village. The Beerappa festival, or Pedda Panduga, celebrated once every five years, is the most significant event in Kuruma life, more cherished than even Sri Rama Navami, the festival of Lord Rama's marriage celebrated by other Hindus.

However, much of the Beerappa story, like many oral traditions, has been altered over time by external influences. I have undertaken the task of translating and retelling this story to preserve its essence and to correct misinterpretations that have arisen due to the changing social and historical contexts. These changes reflect not only the passage of time but also the dominance of other groups who have influenced how our history is told.

Two folk stories that have been passed down particularly stand out as problematic when we reflect on them today.

The first story suggests that the Kurumas trace their origins to Mallanna, a deity assigned to the shepherds. This story tells of Mallanna accidentally burning an ant-hill where two sheep, sheltered by Goddess Parvati, resided. Oppressed by the heat, the sheep emerged and sought Mallanna's protection,  and, reluctantly, he consented. This narrative implies a forced relationship between the

Kurumas and their god, as if they were assigned to him by chance rather than by cultural and spiritual evolution.

Upon critical reflection, this story does not align with the true pride, depth, and dignity of the Kuruma people. It seems to reflect external influences and an attempt to diminish our historical importance by reducing our origins to fables that are inconsistent with the stature of Beerappa. When considered retrospectively, especially in the context of the cultural and religious evolution of the Kurumas, these stories do not sound correct or appropriate. They cast our identity in a passive or subservient light, rather than reflecting the agency and strength that the Kuruma community has historically exhibited.

The truth is that Beerappa, and the Kuruma people, have a much richer, more complex history that deserves to be preserved and celebrated. In human evolution, the domestication of goats, widely acknowledged as the first domesticated animal, marks a pivotal moment in the history of civilization, and the Kuruma people, as shepherds, played a significant role in this transition. Yet, modern educated Kurumas, particularly those who have moved to cities, often refer to themselves as Yadavs, perhaps unaware of the distinct and proud cultural history that sets them apart.

I believe it is essential to retell the Beerappa story accurately, shedding the misinterpretations of the past and bring forth the true cultural significance of our traditions. Beerappa is not only the god of shepherds but also a symbol of strength, resilience, and unity for the Kuruma people. His festival, with its seven-day celebration culminating in the marriage (*lagnam*), is the grandest expression of our communal identity, with rituals such as the sacrifice of a sheep carried on the shoulders of a family member around the temple.

I have drawn great inspiration from my Guru, Professor Kanch Ilaiah, whose work has deepened my understanding of the importance of preserving the cultural identities of marginalized communities. This book is dedicated to him, and I hope it serves as a means to reclaim and honor our heritage. Moreover, I was fortunate to meet Dr. Ostad Oggu Ravi, and together, we aim to bring the Oggu Katha, Dolu, and Patalu traditions to a global audience, ensuring that our culture is celebrated not just in India but across the world.

Though I am a software engineer living in the UK, my heart remains deeply connected to my roots. During a recent visit to India,

I was honored to receive the **Gongidi** from H. Gurunand, Assistant Professor, as a symbol of our shared heritage. It is my hope that this book will be a bridge for future generations, helping them understand the true depth of our cultural history and the importance of Beerappa's legacy.

**Subhash Manthri**
Translator
Email: sbmanthri@gmail.com
Mobile: +447799876931

# Beerappa

# Historical and Cultural Hero

# Beerappa

Vosikeri, deeply feeling a pull from something intangible yet profoundly familiar, decided to return to his hometown. After years of searching for this elusive connection, he finally embarked on a journey that would bring him back to his roots. Boarding a train from Tirupati, he gazed out of the window, lost in the rhythmic clatter of the wheels, his mind diving into a bag of childhood memories.

He remembered that he left the house when he got a job and later got married in to a new home. There are no recount of him having much contact with his hometown or family after that.

The village of Gondipalli is somewhere at the bottom of the records in Anantapur district. Not only in records but also in development and usage, it remains backward. The village is surrounded by hills, slopes, and twisted paths, with trees bending in the wind. The environment is barren, and you wouldn't even know it was there until you stepped into it. If there is no need of connection with someone from that place, there is no reason of a visit.

The village is a home to hundreds of families. All of them are Gorlu kase kurubas, and like them, there are also Boyakulas, Madigalas, and Komats, with no other castes living there. Half of the people farm crops under the lake, while the others work as laborers. The *Mushtikovela* Cheruve is their main source of livelihood. Hills and slopes surround the entire village, and whatever water flows down from those hills and slopes has to eventually make its way into *Mushtikovela* Lake.

Encircled by hills, Gondipalli's unique topography ensures that every drop of water from the surrounding peaks flows directly into Mushtikovela, nurturing the fields and sustaining life in the village. This connection between the land and its people is deeply ingrained, each hill and valley playing a silent yet pivotal role in their existence. The lake, more than just a body of water, stands as a symbol of resilience and sustenance, a mirror of the community's spirit.

Vosikeri's return to Gondipalli is not just a homecoming; it is a reconnection with a forgotten chapter of his life and a community that still holds the echoes of his childhood. As he steps off the train, he carries with him not just his memories but also the weight of the legacy of his people, hoping to rediscover what it means to belong to a place that time and progress have largely overlooked.

In Gondipalli, two crops are grown annually, with paddy being the predominant crop. As you look around, you'll notice heaps of paddy and people engaged in the toil of farming. However, if someone needs an item for any purpose, it is often difficult to find it locally, even with significant effort. Goods valued at ten rupees might be sold at a steep discount, but the challenge lies in bringing these goods to the village, as there is no established supply chain. The villagers do not expect anything to be handed to them; they are self-reliant and supportive of one another, embracing a simple lifestyle that remains untainted by modern pollution, much like their natural surroundings.

## The Journey to Gondipalli

A bus connects Dharmavaram to Mushtikovela, and it operates at an unusual schedule. The bus departs early in the morning from Dharmavaram, before most people are awake. By the time it arrives at Mushtikovela, the villagers are just starting their day. For those who miss the bus or forget their tasks, they have no choice but to postpone them to the next day. Sometimes, people become so absorbed in their work that they lose track of time, and when they realize the bus has arrived, they hastily grab their belongings and rush to catch it, often dressing on the bus itself. This rush sometimes leads to minor scuffles, as the first driver of the bus becomes the target of everyones complaints.

Riding the bus is an adventure of its own. The movement of the bus serves as an impromptu make up session, with the bouncing and jolting, ones appearance changes drastically. The dust and grime from the ride often leave passengers looking as if they've had an unplanned makeover, with faces turned pale and hair streaked with strange shades of white and grey. These natural "cosmetics" are not found in any market, and though passengers might carry small mirrors, they often find no satisfaction in their appearance.

This bus, however, is not just a mode of transportation it becomes a lively, chaotic space, with children playing and passengers voicing their frustrations. Complaints to the driver about his carelessness are common: Oh, you are the driver! Can you drive carefully? You're going to knock down the pole in the middle! Despite their grievances, the community relies heavily on this bus service, as politicians and leaders have largely ignored the need for better roads and infrastructure. They claim to be leaders of the people, but their lack of attention to these basic necessities speaks volumes.

After alighting from the bus, the journey doesn't inspire enthusiasm but rather a sense of resignation. Life in Gondipalli is not as glamorous as working in a call center or participating in the bustling network that controls the Parliament. Here, even basic communication through cell phones is a challenge; the signal is elusive, often requiring individuals to climb trees or find specific spots to get a decent connection. Conversations are brief and filled with misunderstanding, and speaking freely on the phone is rarely an option.

From Gondipalli, the nearest notable place is Chennekottapally, but the journey to Gondipalli feels as arduous as a pilgrimage to Hampi. Missing the bus to Mushtikovela can cause profound frustration, and if a travel encounters an adversary during the long walk, tensions can escalate dangerously.

The distance from Chennekottapalli to Gondipalli is fifteen kilometers, and the path is fraught with challenges. Travelleres must navigate potholes, uneven terrain, and sharp stones that jolt both the body and the spirit. Riding a motorbike on these roads is akin to an endurance test, with every bump and jolt threatening to disrupt one's journey.

Fortunately, recent improvements have made the roads slightly more bearable, sparing travellers from some of the worst potholes and obstacles. However, the struggle remains a constant reminder of the village's isolated existence and the resilience of its people, who continue to endure the challenges of their environment with unwavering determination.

The journey to Gondipalli is fraught with challenges, even with the presence of motorbikes here and there for commuting. The condition of the roads makes every trip an ordeal. Those who have experienced it often wonder if such roads can still exist in this era, where progress is seen in many places. It's said that thieves might find it easy to steal in the night, but escaping from the area is another story entirely due to the treacherous paths.

## Nagamma's Struggles in Gondipalli

As Vosikeri traveled, he found himself lost in a maze of thoughts. When night fell, he and his wife, Nagamma, ate their meal quietly, each absorbed in their own cellphone screens. The glow of their devices was the only light in the compartment, and their interaction was limited to the digital realm. Whether laughing or crying, their emotions were confined to the tiny screens, and they rarely spoke directly to each other. As the clock struck past eleven, Vosikeri gently put his phone aside, hoping to get some sleep. The train moved forward, mirroring the silent aspirations and struggles of the middle class.

As they neared Dharmavaram, Vosikeri and Nagamma woke up early and packed their belongings. The train pulled into the second platform, and an announcement in Telugu echoed through the station, confirming their arrival via the Tirupati Dharmavaram route. Despite the early hour, the platform was alive with activity; vendors hustled through the windows selling all sorts of wares. They hawked idlis, samosas, newspapers, and jasmine flowers, their cries competing with the blaring microphone announcements. The vendors' relentless pace made Vosikeri feel like he was caught in a whirlwind of energy.

They slowly made their way from the station, took an auto to the bus stand, and from there caught a bus to Chennekottapalli (CK Palli). However, they were too late; the bus to Mushtikovela had already departed. They faced the all too familiar plight of missing a critical connection. What can you do? Vosikeri thought, resigning himself to the luck of catching the next bus or finding an auto. Looking down the road to Gondipalli, he saw it strewn with craters and potholes, like scars on torn fabric remnants of countless neglected promises.

After a long wait, an auto finally arrived, and they clambered in awkwardly. The ride was rough; Nagamma clutched onto anything she could to steady herself, her anxiety growing with each jolt. The auto bounced and swayed, causing her head to hit the top with every bump. By the time they finally reached their destination, Nagamma had vented her frustration at both her husband and anyone else in earshot. She cursed the lack of basic facilities, questioning the point of living in such conditions when comfort seemed perpetually out of reach. Her tirade continued as they walked along the edge of Mushtikovela lake, cursing fate for the lack of even the most basic comforts.

The two trudged along the banks of the lake, with Gondipalli still three kilometers away. As they walked, Vosikeri's mind wandered back to memories of Beerappa, the historical and cultural hero whose life stories he had grown up hearing. He recalled the tales of resilience and the communal spirit that had defined Beerappa's life and deeds, feeling a strange comfort in these old recollections. Occasionally, he would chuckle to himself, lost in the vivid images of Beerappa's legendary feats.

Nagamma, noticing his distraction, snapped at him, "What's so funny? Are you mad, laughing by yourself like this? Watch where you're going, you'll trip and fall." Her voice was filled with exasperation, a mix of worry and annoyance as she tried to keep pace with him on the uneven path. Yet, amidst her complaints, there was an unspoken bond a shared struggle that, despite the hardships, kept them moving forward together, step by weary step, toward Gondipalli.

Nagamma has never felt any desire to visit her in laws' village. It's not just her; many women from their own villages feel the same, dreading the journey there. Yet, despite the discomfort, these women are deeply invested in raising daughters, with an inherent belief that the difficulties of life are worth enduring if it means bringing life into the world. However, for many young women, the thought of visiting that village feels like an impossible task too far, too isolated, and too disconnected from the rest of the world. And when they are forced to make the trip, they often curse their husbands throughout the entire journey.

For Vosikeri, returning to his village after so many years felt like a rescue, as if he were a child freed from the clutches of kidnappers. As he neared the village, he was overwhelmed with emotions he couldn't quite express. The connection he had with the land of his birth ran deeper than any other bond and stepping onto that soil felt like a long awaited reunion with a lover's first embrace. There's something uniquely intoxicating about the scent of one's homeland, something that stirs the soul like the fragrance of flowers offered by a lover. For Vosikeri, this return brought forth all those feelings, as if the very soil was welcoming him home after years of separation.

This sense of belonging isn't unique to Vosikeri; it is something everyone should feel. When a person connects with the land of their birth, it becomes part of their identity, a reminder of where they came from and what shaped them. It is only this connection, the bond with one's own soil, that reveals the true essence of a person. Vosikeri, more than anyone else, felt this pull now. He realized that the village, despite its changes, was still a part of him.

As he entered the village, his heart swelled with anticipation, but not everyone recognized him right away. Many of his old friends, those who had spent countless hours playing and working with him, had grown older and struggled to recognize the man he had become. Some remembered but couldn't express it in words hesitant, perhaps, to acknowledge the passage of time. Yet, despite his long absence, Vosikeri greeted everyone he met, whether they remembered him or not. He had always been a solitary figure, someone driven by the desire to study hard and achieve great things, and it was that ambition that had propelled him away from the village.

It had taken fifty-five long years for the fires of ambition, the pursuit of industry and wealth, to finally cool within him. Returning to the village was like meeting long lost relatives after an eternity apart. The village, with its old and new faces, seemed both familiar and foreign to him now.

Even his parents had not seen him in nearly six years. They had grown old, unable to do much for themselves. They no longer took much food and spent their days lying on rugs infront of the house. When they first saw Vosikeri, they couldn't quite believe it was him. For a moment, they squinted, unsure if this was their son or a stranger. But soon, they recognized him. His mother, Naramma, still heartbroken over the long years without her son, expressed her sadness, telling him that even when they called out for their children, none of them had come.

Narappa, his father, in a half-resigned tone, remarked, "What more can you tell me about the passing years?" The years had been hard on them. As Vosikeri's eldest son, Ramanji, stood by with the family, Narappa spoke again, "Isn't it because of you all that we're still alive? What is left to survive here in  Manur?" Even as he said this, his words carried the weight of years of loneliness and longing for his children.

Vosikeri's second brother, however, was more pragmatic. He asked, "Why should we leave if things are fine? You were able to study in Manur; why give up everything and go?" He sought to remind Vosikeri that, despite the hardships, there was still something valuable about staying connected to their roots.

Rangaiah, a close family member, tried to reassure him, "Don't worry, don't worry. Everything will be fine."

Despite all the changes, the village still celebrated its traditions. Everyone in Anantapur would gather for the Gudikatla celebrations, and all the relatives, even those who had never met before, would come together. These festivals were a testament to the enduring strength of family and community bonds, something that remained unchanged despite the passage of time.

As Vosikeri reconnected with his past and his family, the weight of the years melted away, and he realized that, no matter how far he had travelled, the land, the village, and his people would always be a part of him.

# The Gudikatla Festival Begins

The Gudikatla celebrations, once a forgotten tradition, had now transformed into a grand event, attracting Kurubas from all over to gather in Anantapur. Even Vosikerappa, who had come for two important reasons, was among the attendees. First, he had a project nearing its deadline, one he had long worked on and was about to submit. Second, he had made a personal vow to offer silver horses to the house deity if his wishes were fulfilled.

As preparations for the festival intensified, Ramanji, the eldest in the household, ensured that all the visiting relatives were taken care of. He brought rice and food to the guests, who gathered around the water tub in front of the house to wash their hands and feet, signaling the start of the meal. As some sat to eat and others served, Vosikeri and Nagamma chose to step aside and wander quietly in the verandah, not engaging with the commotion.

For Nagamma, nothing about her in laws' village appealed to her. While she had no issues with other villages or their people, something about her husband's village deeply irked her. She could never warm up to the people, nor did she enjoy the customs of visiting, mingling, or even speaking to the family there. There was a sense of disdain that welled up inside her whenever she interacted with her mother in law's village. Despite the villagers' simplicity and purity, free from the corruption of worldly desires, Nagamma found herself disgusted. The people lived humbly, never relying on others, never lazy, always feeding any guests with genuine affection. But for Nagamma, this open heartedness felt overwhelming, almost suffocating.

The villagers, unpretentious and generous, saw hospitality as their way of life. For them, even unexpected guests were welcomed with open arms and treated with utmost care and love. To Nagamma, however, this felt alien, contrasting sharply with her upbringing. Her philosophy was the opposite: she spoke her mind without reservation, never hiding her opinions behind pleasantries. She believed in being direct and blunt, even if it meant offending others. This made her stand apart from the village community, and it left her feeling disconnected.

Nagamma had never been particularly close to her relatives, nor had she shown any real fondness for them. Her father, Kittappa, had raised her in a way that emphasized self-reliance and emotional distance. Kittappa was a man who valued isolation; he took all necessary precautions to prevent any relatives from visiting his home. Even though he hailed from Chittoor district, he had long severed any connection with his native place, living as though the entire world was washed away, leaving only him and his immediate family. He believed in the simplicity of family: a household consisting of a husband, wife, and their children. For him, money was the only thing that mattered, the one tool that could solve all problems.

Nagamma, raised in this manner, felt uneasy when faced with large gatherings of people. The warmth of her in laws' village was overwhelming to her, and she had no interest in maintaining relationships or interacting with extended family. This distance and disinterest in socializing became a pattern in her marriage, with neither she nor Vosikeri allowing many relatives into their lives.

Despite Nagamma's frustrations, Vosikeri was lost in nostalgia. He led his wife into a familiar grove, smiling as memories of his childhood flooded back. He pointed out the small stone built chavidi and the shrines for Beerappa, showing her the places that held meaning for him. He spoke of the games he played in the forest, recalling how he had injured himself countless times by falling from trees or getting scratched by branches. His smile reflected the joy of those simple days.

As the Beerappa festival (Parsa) approached, Vosikeri shared with Nagamma the excitement that used to fill the air during those days. He described the lively celebrations at *Chintopu*, where he and his friends would gather to revel in the festivities.

Seeing Beerappa swamy's form in the grove a majestic figure with a mustache, machete, staff, barge, *dalavaithali* (a curved weapon), sword, and the utsavamurthy (festival deity) Nagamma felt a sense of calm wash over her. Beerappa 's presence was formidable yet reassuring, a reminder of the power and strength the deity embodied. For a brief moment, Nagamma's inner turmoil quieted, as she stood before the mighty figure, feeling a connection to something greater. It was as if the sight of Beerappa softened her disdain, offering her a glimpse into the reverence and tradition that her husband cherished so deeply.

Though the festival carried the weight of history and culture, it also marked a significant moment for both Vosikeri and Nagamma a chance for them to reconcile with their pasts and each other, surrounded by the very traditions that had shaped their lives, whether they embraced them fully or not.

Vosikeri's heart softened as he stood before the form of Beerappa, the deity who held a revered place in his life. The rigidness that had built up over the years seemed to melt away, and something deep within him disappeared in that moment. It reminded him of Adidev, the primordial god, and how Beerappa too had become a powerful figure in his spiritual journey.

As he shared childhood memories with his wife, Nagamma, a playful nostalgia filled the air. He talked about the village temple, recalling how he and other children would cut colorful papers to decorate for the festivals, using flour to paste them on the walls. He even remembered Angalasappa, a local character who would travel to town to fetch tin puris, bright colored paper used for decorations. Sometimes, Vosikeri would pocket a piece of paper or two, just for fun.

"Angalasappa is a strange name," Nagamma commented, smiling at the memory.

"Don't get mad if I tell you about Ayyappa," Vosikeri teased.

Nagamma, in her usual practical manner, replied, "What's there to say about Ayyappa? There's no difference between him and the others. They all seem the same, whether they're serious or just another boy."

But her quip soon shifted to a playful accusation, You, Vosikeri, with all your stories, are you telling me your thieving ways are gone?

"Thief? No, Nagamma, my father never cheated or stole a single rupee from anyone," Vosikeri defended himself. He reminisced about how his father used to walk through the fields in the middle of the night, collecting debts for sacrifices when the crops were harvested. "It was because of his hard work and honesty that we reached this level," he added proudly.

Nagamma, unmoved, quipped, "Oh dear, it wasn't honesty that saved you. You studied hard and got a job. That's what made the difference, not your father's honesty."

"Whatever you may think," Vosikeri replied, "but inside, you know the truth. I worked hard, and it was for you and our children. I gave my life to this family."

Nagamma's face softened slightly, though her words remained sharp. "You're not the only one. Everyone sacrifices for their families. Whether you liked it or not, this is your glory now. Everyone does it."

Vosikeri's voice grew more pained as he continued, "I wanted to get a good job to support my parents and younger siblings. And I did that. I focused on my career. But after you came into my life, I had to leave everything behind. I couldn't be there for my siblings the way I wanted to. I couldn't greet them; I couldn't even help them when they needed me. I buried my desires, hoping that if my children were okay, then I would be okay."

Tears welled in his eyes as he reflected on his sacrifices. "By God's grace, both of our children are well educated, and I believe they'll settle down soon. That's the only happiness left in my life." He wiped the tears with a handkerchief, feeling the weight of his unfulfilled responsibilities to his parents and his village.

"I couldn't do anything for my parents or my village. In the end, I've become a stranger in my own land. A stranger to my family, and even a stranger in my own home." He looked at Nagamma, his voice heavy with emotion, "This is what I've earned in my life, after all these years."

Nagamma, pragmatic as always, brushed aside his sorrow. "What can you do if you don't have money in hand? Everyone is selfish. Whether they shower you with flowers or forget your name, it doesn't matter. Because you left, we've lost connection with a few stones along the way, but life goes on. These people will die wrapped in their own problems, just like everyone else."

She softened for a moment, realizing the depth of his pain. "But still, it hurts to know that you've lost touch with your own place of birth, your parents. That's no small thing, but it's not your fault. It's just the way life turned out. Let it go," she said, her voice filled with a rare sense of comfort.

Vosikeri, despite his lingering pain, nodded. He knew deep down that Nagamma was right. The burden of responsibility had steered him away from the very roots he cherished. But now, standing before Beerappa and reflecting on his life, he felt both the loss and the fulfillment of the path he had chosen. All he could do now was make peace with the choices of his past and embrace the hope that his children's future would bring the fulfillment he had once sought for himself.

A week before the Beerappa Jatra, a soft flag woven from Unni is hoisted on the flagpole infront of the temple as part of Beerappa's custom. Vosikerappa, aware of the tradition, murmured, "This is the beginning of Beerappa 's Parasa kadukada, isn't it?"

"Yes," Poojarappa replied, "Beerappa is the main god of the Kurubas, and this is why we raise the flag. All these customs go back to him, and the tradition originates with him."

Nagamma, still fuming but curious, asked, "Is it Poojarappa who's raising that flag?"

"Yes," Poojarappa replied, "As soon as the flag is raised, everyone knows that *Parasa* has begun. Even though we live scattered in the hills, our villages were founded on these customs. We raise the flag before Beerappa comes to Aevur. Later, even kings adopted this system."

Vosikerappa nodded, adding, "Beerappa is our king as well. That's why the flag flutters before Beerappa *Parasa*. From the day the flag is hoisted, various activities begin in Manur(Village). Cotton spinners, wool spinners, and others who participate in these rituals get to work. Even those who are yet to marry observe this time with respect, as it signals the start of Beerappa 's festival."

The tradition of raising the flag brought a sense of unity to the village, and as it fluttered in the wind, it carried with it the deep roots of their shared heritage. Though tensions and frustrations existed within the family, the flag reminded them all the strength and resilience of their customs.

In the village, the traditions of Beerappa 's festival transcend caste, uniting everyone as brothers and sisters. The customs, such as the Beerappa Paras, are not exclusive to the Kuruba community but embraced by people of all castes in the village. They come together without division, whether they are farmers, laborers, or craftsmen, adhering to their village's ancient practices. The *Beerappa Gudikatlu*, the feast held during the festival, ensures that meals are provided for everyone for two days, following a custom observed in every village where Kurubas reside.

Pujarappa explained that the meals are prepared in a large vessel called an *Anda*, enough to feed the entire village. On the second day, after worshiping Lingadeva and Beerappa, the villagers cook and distribute the *Taligibuvva* (offering) from this large vessel. The tradition has always included every member of the village, although a discriminatory practice involves giving the last of the food to the Madiga community by placing it on plates separately. Vosikerappa remarked that this practice of separation should be abolished, emphasizing the need for equality among all people.

Nagamma, curious about the grand procession, asked, "Is this Pujarappa's palanquin, and is it made as grandly in the towns?"

Pujarappa responded, "Yes, this is Pallakinamma. In the towns, whoever wants to come and eat can join. But here, we carry Beerappa on the palanquin and parade him around the entire village, with music and festivities. It's a true celebration."

Nagamma noticed another structure and inquired, "What's this thin palanquin next to it?"

Pujarappa explained, "This is the *Galipallaki*, a smaller palanquin brought ahead of Beerappa 's procession. It's carried by two people and serves as a kind of trial run before the grand procession. It prepares the path for Beerappa *Parasa*, ensuring everything goes smoothly."

Vosikeri, still processing the details, asked, "What exactly is a palanquin, Pujarappa? Isn't it like a cradle?"

Pujarappa elaborated, "The palanquin, or ***pallaki***, comes from ancient traditions. It's made of hard wood, similar to a crib. Above it is an arch, where the deity sits. Two long pieces of wood stretch underneath to carry the palanquin. It even has a bell attached. Two people at the back and two in the front carry it. Before Beerappa sits in the palanquin, he's dressed in silk robes and prepared for the journey through the village."

Nagamma asked, "Will the villagers carry our god in the procession?"

Pujarappa nodded, "Yes, certain households in the village have the responsibility of carrying Beerappa 's palanquin. Only they are allowed to do so. And because Beerappa is a shepherd god, the Dalavai his chosen representative wears special sandals when walking in the procession."

Curious about the Dalavai, Vosikeri asked, "What is this *Dalavai*, Pujarappa? Is this a tradition from Tirupati?"

Pujarappa explained, "The Dalavai wears a special gold chain called Dalavaithali, with a pendant in the middle like a dollar. When the Dalavai wears this chain, he's no longer considered just a man but becomes a representation of the god himself. As he carries the palanquin, he cries out as if possessed by the god's spirit. A silver umbrella is also carried above the Dalavai. While some umbrellas are not made of silver, the Dalavai has the privilege of carrying the one that is. Only a select few have the honor of accepting the role of Dalavai during the procession."

Nagamma, still reflecting on the explanation, asked, "So, is there a distinction among the Kuruba community about who can be a Dalavai?"

Pujarappa reassured her, "No, there's no hierarchy or discrimination among the Kurubas. The Dalavai is chosen based on availability and tradition. It's not about status or division but about fulfilling a sacred role for Beerappa during the festival. Whoever is available at the time takes on the responsibility, and it's an honor to be part of the procession."

Through these traditions, the village maintains its unity and reverence for Beerappa, ensuring that everyone, regardless of caste or background, participates in and honors the god together. The palanquin procession, the Dalavai's role, and the collective feasts serve as symbols of the village's shared heritage, binding the community through their faith and customs.

Vosikerappa, clearly unsettled by the conversation, reflected on the ongoing internal divisions within the Kuruba community. "If they keep following the same old methods but still differentiate themselves within the same caste, where does harmony come from?" he asked. "That's why *Kurubollu* are always in conflict. When there's so much discrimination within the same caste, how can there ever be unity? It's hard for outsiders to understand why these things persist. If the elders are fighting like this, how can we expect the younger generations to change? They just follow the customs they're taught."

Nagamma nodded, "All these traditions were passed down from the elders, and it's not just in one caste. Every caste has its customs, and there are always variations within them."

Exactly, Pujarappa added. Caste as a whole may seem unified, but within it, there are all these differences and distinctions.

Vosikerappa sighed, "Yes, Pujarappa, times have changed. Shouldn't these practices change too? It's not enough to just meet the expectations of caste customs while ignoring the issues created by these differences."

Pujarappa pondered for a moment and responded, "Ah, but this is the way things have always been, Vosikeri. These traditions run deep."

Vosikerappa shifted the conversation, "You mentioned Beeradev has a lot of friends. Tell me more about that."

Pujarappa explained, "There is a custom involving *Alugollu*, a ritual warrior who sharpens both sides of his sword and engages in a ritual duel with two swords. It's called Kattalagu. The Dalavai stands on the rocks, watching. *Mundlapallaki* is about the Dalavai's role. There's a belief that children will grow up to be heroes if they apply *Bhandaru* (sacred ash) to their foreheads. However, girls don't come near the sharp knives during the ritual. The *Iragals* men who stick pointed wooden rods into their bellies are also part of the procession."

Nagamma, wincing at the thought, asked sarcastically, "Oh, doesn't it hurt? Are you still stuck in the stone age with these traditions? Iragalla or Veeragalla?"

Pujarappa chuckled softly but defended the tradition, "The Beerappa Jatra can't happen without the Veeragallu warriors of the festival. They are essential to the tradition. They dress in white, don't wear a cloak, tie a white handkerchief around their heads, and wear garlands of flowers around their necks. Their bodies are covered in Vibhuti (sacred ash), and they carry Bhandaru on their foreheads while holding a fork in hand."

He continued, "There's also a divine ritual at night called Beerappa Meravani. Experienced devotees craft a meter long stick wrap new cloth one end and , and once lit, they bow in four directions before offering the stick to Beerappa to begin the worship. When the cloth dries, they sprinkle kerosin on it. Once the divine service concludes, the Beerappa procession begins. There's a tradition where devotees must bow to the deity and to Bhudevi (Earth Goddess). After the divine service is completed, Dasappa blows the conch shell, and Goravayya beats his drum, signaling the start of the procession."

Nagamma, still processing all this, asked, "And what's the significance of the black carpet?"

Pujarappa explained, "The *Kambali* (black woolen blanket) has a sacred place in these rites. It's part of the Palamatastu tradition, which relates to religious rituals and rites of passage. Beerappa is seated on this blanket, and an *abhishekam* (ritual anointing) is done with milk as an offering. Alongside Beerappa, we also worship *Revana Siddeshwara* and *Siddaramaiah*, who spread their teachings among the people. The Kambali is always used in these religious rituals for the Pala community."

Nagamma, intrigued, asked, "What exactly is *Palamatam*?"

Pujarappa smiled, "*Palamatam* isn't just about milk. It's the practice of sharing everything with the gods. In the old days, people would first offer a portion of their harvest, game, or food to the gods. 'This is for this god, that is for that god, this is for *Bhumamma* (Earth Goddess), and this is for the people of the village.' It was a tradition of giving before taking anything for oneself. The idea of sharing was instilled by the elders. They believed in dividing everything among the gods and the people before taking for themselves."

Vosikerappa, deep in thought, responded, "That custom of sharing is one of the few things that keeps the community connected. But it's important that we don't let these divisions whether through caste or outdated customs hinder the unity we need."

Pujarappa nodded in agreement, understanding the tension between tradition and the need for change. The community's history and rituals were deeply rooted, yet the modern world demanded a rethinking of how they approached these ancient practices. The challenge, as always, lay in balancing respect for the past with the evolving expectations of the future.

Pujarappa began explaining the deep-rooted traditions of the Pala religion, which is considered the faith of cowherds. He said, "The Pala religion represents purity, as its followers are pure hearted, just like milk. The cowherds are simple people who do not know evil. They live in harmony with nature and are untainted by the complexities of the world."

After this, Pujarappa moved on to describe the significance of drums in their traditions. He recalled a story that Vosikeri had heard from his grandmother, a tale that revolved around Dollu and a demon named Dollasura. Vosikeri was apprehensive about what Pujarappa might say next, especially since Dollu was such a central part of their folklore. But the story captivated Nagamma, who urged Vosikeri to share it.

Pujarappa recounted the tale: "The demon Dollasura performed a terrifying penance to please Lord Shiva. Impressed by his devotion, Shiva granted him a boon. But instead of asking for worldly riches or power, *Dollasura* wanted Shiva to abandon his responsibilities and stay in *Dollasura* stomach , staying in his womb forever. Shiva, bound by his promise, allowed it. However, without Shiva's presence, chaos ensued in Kailasa and on Earth, as the demon, now empowered by Shiva's blessing, caused havoc."

Seeing the disorder in both worlds, Parvati, Shiva's consort, ordered Nandi, Shiva's divine bull, to put an end to it. She instructed Nandi to tear open Dollasura's stomach and release Shiva. Nandi did as commanded, ripping the demon's belly and freeing Shiva. In his rage, Shiva flayed the demon's skin and used it to create a drum. He tied the skin of Dollasura to both sides of the drum and began playing it. This is why drums are an integral part of Beerappa 's temple rituals, and *Damaruka*, a small drum, holds such importance. In ancient times, shepherds used these drums to ward off wild animals, and even today, drums are made from goat skin, continuing the tradition."

Nagamma, skeptical, asked, "Did Shiva really go inside the demon's stomach? How does a god not know the end?"

Pujarappa chuckled softly. "God knows everything, and stories like this were woven by the folk to explain the mysteries of divine power and to relieve the exhaustion from their daily labor. In the past, stories and songs were the primary sources of entertainment and a way to pass time. While such tales may seem strange now, they served a vital purpose back then."

He then described other objects used in Beerappa 's rituals. "The Chamaram, a fan used to cool Beerappa, is made from either the hair of a chameleon or the Kadauventriku of animal. A special stick, adorned with silver leaves, is used to wave this fan in front of Beerappa during the procession. Special families are tasked with this sacred duty."

Pujarappa continued, "Another important object is a lion's face, made from five metals. It plays a key role in the procession as well. The *Beerappa Danda* is a sacred garland worn by Beera Dev, and a sacred knot is tied to the hands of the attendant carrying the garland. Dalavai also holds something made of silver in his hand, which is similar to that sacred knot. It must never be put down and is treated with utmost reverence."

He then mentioned the **Sitala**, small clay pots made by potters. These pots, when brought to the temple, are first blessed by the priest before being used in the rituals. The process of making and using these sacred objects is steeped in tradition, with the pots brought in a ceremonial procession to the temple. Pujarappa added that the Binde, or sacred pots, are specifically meant for Beerappa 's daughters. They contain an urn and two mugitas and are always brought in a bamboo basket by the grandparents of the family. Rudrakshas are placed on Beerappa 's altar, and a conch shell sits nearby to complete the rituals.

Nagamma curiously asked Pujarappa about the meaning of "Mariseethalbinde." Pujarappa responded with an old story passed down by the elders. He began, saying there once lived a shepherd named Muddalinga on a hill in the forests of Srisailam, where he tended his sheep. Back then, the present-day Mallanna temple was just a small shrine. Muddalinga, who, would worship Mallanna, praying for protection from wild animals and thieves. Every morning, he would take a pitcher to fetch water from a nearby river. He called this pitcher **"Sitala,"** a vessel that could hold water deep inside. Over time, **"Sitala"** became known as "Patala."

Muddalinga would use that water along with flowers and whatever else he could find to offer his worship. One day, Muddalinga met another shepherd named Devappa. Devappa, who lived in Bandigutta village, had a habit of drinking alcohol. However, he was notorious for not paying for his drinks on time, often demanding more from liquor sellers without settling his dues. This caused frequent conflicts, and one day, the people in the village caught him and roughed him up. Devappa managed to escape and, in his desperation, threw a stone at them. The stone fell without hitting anyone, but when it landed, it cracked open, revealing a sparkling, gold-like shimmer.

It was then that everyone realized the stone contained gold. From that day forward, people were more than happy to provide Devappa with all the alcohol he wanted, hoping to discover more about the source of the stone. They continuously asked him where it came from and who gave it to him, believing Devappa knew something important. Devappa eventually gave the stone to Muddalinga, but he kept quiet about its origins, leaving people wondering.

As the story goes, one day Devappa encountered Muddalinga again. This time, Muddalinga appeared exhausted and worn, with his throat parched and dry. When Devappa asked what had happened, Muddalinga painfully explained that thieves had stolen all his sheep. From that day forward, Muddalinga wandered the hills of Srisailam. When Devappa invited him to his home, Muddalinga promised to visit on Diwali Amavasya (the new moon of Diwali).

When Diwali Amavasya arrived, Muddalinga appeared at Devappas home, just as promised. Word spread throughout Bandigutta that Muddalinga had arrived, and the villagers rushed to his house to bow at his feet. They adorned him with flowers and carried him in a palanquin. However, a local religious teacher from Adevur, who witnessed the scene, began to protest. He questioned why the villagers were worshiping Muddalinga instead of him, a local priest. The teacher threatened to cast them out of the Kuruba caste if they continued.

Fearing the consequences of being ostracized, the villagers asked for forgiveness. Devappa, however, stood firm, insisting that Muddalinga was the one he revered. In response, the priest decreed that Devappa must live in a cave far away in Chiruthalavan. Though Devappa was frightened, he complied with the order and took refuge in the cave, which was filled with scorpions and snakes.

Muddalinga, knowing Devappa's situation, came to his aid by sprinkling bandaru (sacred ash) on the snakes and scorpions, rendering them harmless to Devappa. Even the seven-headed cobra that resided there could not harm him. Meanwhile, the priest, who would bathe in a nearby river every day, encountered a cow drinking from the river. In anger, the priest struck the cow, causing it to collapse. Horrified by the sin of cow slaughter, the priest was tormented with guilt.

Seeing his suffering, Devappa left the cave and used Bhandaru sprinkle (a sacred remedy) to heal the cow. The cow immediately stood up, and the priest, realizing his mistake, began treating Devappa with great respect, seeing him as equal to God.

From that day on, people started visiting the places where Muddalinga used to go. Some even ventured to Srisailam in search of gold, while others began worshiping Muddalinga and Mallanna. This story, Pujarappa explained, is where Sitalaguri comes from.

Nagamma, however, was skeptical. She listened to Pujarappa's tale and then questioned, "Is there really such a story behind Sitala? I find it hard to believe all this. Do you really think educated people will accept your stories, Pujarappa?"

Pujarappa smiled gently and replied, "These stories have been passed down for generations. They are more than just myths they carry the essence of our ancestors' beliefs. People may question them now, but they reflect our connection to the divine and the power of faith."

Nagamma, still intrigued, shifted the conversation, "Pujarappa, how often do they change the Dalavai and Iragalla? I've never heard much about the Dalavai. Can you tell us more?"

Pujarappa chuckled at her question, realizing the couple wasn't as familiar with their own traditions as they should be. "Ah, you two are not Kurubollas, it seems," he teased lightly, "or at least, you've forgotten some things about our heritage."

He went on to explain in detail, "The Dalavai is a critical figure in our festivals, the representative of Beerappa himself. The Dalavai changes from time to time, depending on who is chosen to bear the role. The process involves a sacred transformation, as the Dalavai wears the Dalavaithali, a gold chain that symbolizes his connection to Beerappa . While carrying the palanquin, the Dalavai becomes more than just a person he is believed to embody the spirit of Beerappa during the festival. This is why the position of Dalavai is so revered, and why it's passed down carefully, with great respect."

"The Iragalla, or warriors of the festival," he continued, "perform in the procession, symbolizing bravery and the spirit of sacrifice. They carry iron rods, piercing their bellies as a testament to their devotion, much like the trials Beerappa faced in ancient times. These acts of courage are meant to honor the god and keep the connection between the divine and the people alive."

Pujarappa's detailed explanation gave Vosikerappa and Nagamma a deeper understanding of the spiritual significance behind these traditions, even if they still seemed somewhat distant to them. While the stories of Muddulinga and Devappa might feel fantastical, the roles of the Dalavai and Iragalla in the Beerappa Jatra were very real, deeply rooted in the cultural identity of the Kuruba community.

The conversation with Pujarappa became a reflection on culture and tradition. He emphasized the importance of knowing one's roots, saying, "What if we live without knowing our culture? If we don't know who we are, what can we teach our children?"

Nagamma responded with skepticism, suggesting that children today prioritize education over customs. "Pujarappa, children don't seem to care much about caste or traditions nowadays. Maybe they'll learn about these things when they are older," she said.

Pujarappa, however, disagreed. "It may not seem necessary now, but those who ignore traditions will eventually find themselves lost. When it comes to things like marriage, our customs must be followed. It's not something you can set aside," he explained.

Nagamma then quipped, "So, they'll remember these traditions just for marriage? Even if they follow it, they'll have their own ways of doing things."

Pujarappa smiled, "Yes, they may grumble at first, but they will eventually come to appreciate the value of our customs. Take Beerappa 's festival, for instance. Biradeva is carried on a palanquin, accompanied by instruments. The Dalavai walks next to Lingadev Beerappa, and the priest joins the procession. Two attendants carry the palanquin, and they are warrior's heroes in their own right."

He continued explaining the traditions of the Beerappa festival, detailing the role of the *Dalavai*, the chosen representative of

Beerappa . The *Dalavai* is appointed during the Beerappa Peddaparas, which takes place once every fortnight. "God's thali is given to the Dalavai, and this thali is tied around his neck. The Iragals act as Beerappa 's soldiers, piercing iron rods near their navels and chanting 'Suk Sukko Shiva Shiva' during the procession."

Nagamma was surprised at the complexity of these customs. "What happens after the new Dalavai is chosen?" she asked.

Pujarappa replied, "The new *Dalavai* must follow strict rules he can't touch anything made of leather, except for his sandals. He mustn't lie, and he can't travel by bus, lorry, or bicycle. He mustn't eat in anyone's house except his own. If he violates these rules, his title is revoked."

The discussion then moved to the Iragals, who Pujarappa described as Beerappa 's warriors. They wear turbans, carry swords and shields, and adorn their necks with a taittu(Talisman) made of rudrakshas and a half-moon symbol. "If their king dies heroically, the Iragals will swallow the half-moon piece around their necks and follow him in death," he said.

After the *Dalavai i*s chosen, a large feast is held for the village, followed by a festival the next day. The Iragals perform a ritual known as the Gaupike program, where neighboring villagers from Garimekalapally, Acchampally, and others bring their sheep to Beerappa 's temple. In this ritual, a sheep is caught, and the Iragals bite its throat, drinking the blood as a symbolic act.

Nagamma was horrified. "Ayeyyo, Yappa Swami! I'd faint at the sight of all that blood!" she exclaimed.

Pujarappa explained, "It's a ritual, Nagamma. It signifies the shepherds' belief that the more sheep they catch, the better their flock will grow. This is why they perform the ritual it's tied to their livelihood and faith."

The conversation then shifted to Vosikerappa's journey in life. Born to Narayanamma and Kuruba Micheyya's daughter, Vosikerappa was one of nine children. His early life in the village of Mushtikovela was marked by struggle, as the village had no school or facilities, and people often questioned the value of education. Despite this, Vosikerappa walked four to eight kilometers every day to attend school, eventually passing his tenth standard and moving to Anantapur for further studies.

As he progressed in his education, Vosikerappa took on the responsibility of supporting his two younger brothers, cooking for them and ensuring they had the chance to study. His dedication paid off he completed his degree at TTD College in Tirupati and later earned an M.A. and Ph.D. in Anthropology at S.V. University. Vosikerappa's determination not to give up, even in the face of hardship, led him to a successful career as an assistant professor at the same university where he had studied.

Through all their achievements, Vosikerappa and Nagamma remained tied to their traditions, even as they navigated the modern world. They had faced the challenge of balancing their cultural heritage with the demands of contemporary life, just as Pujarappa had warned. Their stories were a testament to the enduring power of culture and the importance of knowing one's roots.

Vosikeri's life had followed a path deeply intertwined with both tradition and modern success. His father-in-law, Kittappa, had arranged his marriage to Nagamma, a bright woman who had already completed her degree in Homeopathy and worked in the Puthalapattu Government Hospital. Nagamma was an intelligent and kind woman, and when Kittappa proposed the marriage, Vosikerappa accepted without hesitation. The wedding took place in Tirupati in the presence of elders from both sides, and after the ceremony, Vosikeri settled entirely in Tirupati with his new family.

His life was seemingly perfect. He had secured a job at a young age, married, and was blessed with twin sons, both intelligent and well educated, having completed their engineering degrees. His sons were now in Delhi, preparing for the Civil Services exam. The family was comfortable, with a home that Kittappa had generously provided. Vosikeri, Nagamma, and their children lived a dignified life, relying on no one.

As Vosikeri neared retirement from his university post, where he worked as an assistant professor, he received approval for a major UGC research project. The project gave him the opportunity to explore his passion researching his own culture, the ancient history of the Kuruba community. He believed that even if a man didn't have material wealth, he still had his caste and heritage, which brought a sense of belonging and pride. Vosikeri reflected, "A person who openly embraces their identity, even if it's through caste, is better than one who denies it while secretly harboring pride."

Vosikeri had always been fascinated by the origins of his community. The Kurubas, an ancient race of shepherds, had a long and storied history, born and raised in the hills, living off the land with their flocks. The time had finally come for him to return to Gondipalli, where he planned to dive deep into this research. It was the Beerappa Parasane, an event he hadn't attended since his school days, that served as the catalyst for this journey. Vosikeri recalled the grand celebration from his childhood and now felt it was the right time to revisit the roots of his culture.

He also reflected on the grandeur of the Gudikatlu ceremonies, which were central to Kuruba heritage. The traditions had been passed down for centuries. In 1336, the founders of the Vijayanagara Empire, Harihara and Bakkaraya, had organized a grand festival at the temples, a gesture that cemented the bond between the Kuruba rulers and the kingdom. Later, Sri Krishna Deva Raya, another prominent Kuruba king, continued the Gudikatlu celebrations in Hampi, showcasing the might and glory of their empire. Though many had heard of these celebrations, the true story behind them remained elusive, even to Vosikeri.

Vosikeri's personal connection to these traditions ran deep. He had made a vow to Beerappa that if his sons succeeded in their studies, he would offer silver horses to the god. Now, with his sons having excelled in their education, he had come to fulfill his promise, bringing beautifully adorned silver horses as an offering to the deity.

The Gudikatlu celebrations were a massive event, drawing Kurubas not just from Andhra Pradesh and Karnataka, but also from abroad. It was said that those who were born into the Kuruba caste but hadn't witnessed the Gudikatlu were seen as lacking in their cultural experience, even labeled as sinners in pamphlets distributed before the event. With more than 350,000 people expected to attend, preparations were in full swing. Anantapur district alone had more than 250 Gudikatlu, and the celebration was expected to bring together people from all corners of the region. The connection between the Kannada and Andhra Kurubas was strong, as both communities crossed borders to participate in each other's festivals.

One custom that piqued Vosikeri's curiosity was the unique tradition of Gudikatlu, which seemed to be exclusive to Anantapur.

As he overheard conversations about this ritual, he grew increasingly eager to uncover the secrets behind it.

The day of the festival arrived, and Biradeva was decorated with great care. A tractor was adorned, and wooden kiridandis (platforms) were prepared to carry the horses. As the celebrations began, the air was filled with the sound of traditional instruments, and the village came alive with the energy of the Gudikatlu ceremony.

Through all of this, Vosiker i  felt a profound connection to his heritage, even as he navigated the complexities of modern life. His return to Gondipalli and his involvement in the Gudikatlu were not just about fulfilling a personal vow  they were part of a larger quest to understand the history and legacy of his people. His research project, coupled with his participation in the Beerappa *Parasane*, represented a merging of the old and the new, tradition and scholarship, and the timeless bond between a man and his culture.

The grand festival for Beerappa was in full swing, and Vosikeri was captivated by the elaborate decorations. The horses, adorned with jasmine garlands and silver umbrellas, were a sight to behold. The *ajawwa* (a cover) was carefully placed over the decorations to protect them from birds or anything else that might spoil the beauty. Each horse had been meticulously adorned with jasmine flowers and silver embellishments. Horseshoes were placed alongside them, while green, silver, and brown horses were arranged to support the bamboo poles that carried along.

Vosikeri stood in awe, almost intoxicated by the scene in front of him. The love and devotion put into decorating the horses, the silver umbrellas, and the sacred bandaru (holy ash) brought a sense of reverence to the atmosphere. The priest took special care in placing the silver horses, made by Vosikerappa, on either side of Beerappa, adding a touch of personal fulfillment to the divine display. Beerappa himself was dressed in a way that symbolized rebirth, like a child emerging from the womb.

The grand procession set off toward Anantapur, with everyone both young and old gathering for the occasion. An open ground of over two hundred acres on Athmakur Road had already been filled with people from various regions: Itikulapallayya, Pedayya, Mushtllappa, Gollapallayya, Vosikerappaswamy, Kurlapallayya, Shettipallayya, and many others from surrounding villages. For six days, it seemed that the locals of Anantapur had vanished, replaced by the influx of Kurubas and those celebrating the Gudikatlu festival.

That night, a program was organized where the history of the Kuruba God Beerappa and the heroic deeds of the Kuruba community were recounted by speakers. The first to speak were Kartanaparthi *Guruvulayah* and Mopurupalli *Guruvulayah*, who shared the local legends about Kuruba history, captivating the audience with their stories.

The listeners, moved by the speeches, chanted "Jai Kuruba, Jai Jai Kuruba" in unison. The energy of the crowd was palpable.

Next, Siddappameti, an 85-year-old folk singer from Karnataka, was invited to perform. Siddappa had been singing about Lingadevara Beerappa since he was just thirteen, dedicating his life to retelling the stories of Beerappa through historical folk songs. His performance stirred deep emotions in the crowd, even though his dialect Kannada from the Gulbarga region was difficult for Vosikeri and others to fully comprehend. Nevertheless, the rhythm and soul of the song resonated with everyone. Some in the audience, feeling the depth of Beerappas hardships through Siddappa's singing, wiped tears from their eyes, moved by the power of the folk tale.

Big screens were set up around the ground, allowing everyone to witness the performances closely. The scenes of people wiping their tears were captured and displayed on the screens, further amplifying the emotional weight of the moment. Vosikeri, though unable to understand every word, tried to write down as much as he could from what hc heard and saw, determined to preserve the experience.

After Siddappa's performance, Maddaiah, a history teacher from Kurnool, took the stage and shared historical facts about the origins of the Kurubas, providing a more academic context to the cultural stories.

Then, Acharya Junjappa, a retired archaeologist from Mysore University, shared his insights, delving into history even older than the Indus civilization. His knowledge spanned across Telugu, Kannada, and English, allowing the audience to grasp the depth of Kuruba history. Junjappa explained how the Kurubas, in their early days, were forest dwellers who survived on tubers, vines, and hunting. The Kuruba people had developed their cultural rituals around hunting and eating the animals they captured, forming a strong connection with the land and nature.

As Vosikeri listened, he diligently wrote down every detail, recognizing the importance of preserving these stories for future generations. This festival was not just a moment of celebration but a reflection of the rich and ancient history of the Kuruba community its resilience, traditions, and the powerful bond between the people and their god Beerappa.

The Kurubas, one of India's ancient communities, have a deep-rooted connection to nature, spirituality, and wisdom. Their origins, culture, and history are often intertwined with the land they lived on caves, hills, and forests and the animals they domesticated.

The term Kuruba has been historically tied to people who lived in caves or hills. Kuru refers to someone who resides in these natural environments, and Kuri means a person skilled at surviving in forests and hills, using intellect to nurture what they found rather than relying solely on hunting. This consciousness, intelligence, and ability to adapt marked the Kuruba people as uniquely connected to nature.

In Kuruba tradition, spiritual development is considered a fundamental aim of life. They believe that chanting Omkara (the sacred syllable Om) symbolizes the revelation of nature's wisdom and becomes a measure of knowledge. Non violence, as a virtue, is deeply ingrained in Kuruba teachings. The Omkara chant, evolving from sounds like Ma and later becoming A+U+M (Om), was seen as a connection to the divine and nature. The call of Aries, symbolizing this wisdom, made the Kurubas early explorers of spirituality.

According to Siddhaiah, a Dharma guru of the Gonds, Kuruba doesn't just refer to a caste or profession; it represents wisdom and spirituality. He likened the role of Kurubas to that of good shepherds, and many Dharmas (faiths) teach wisdom that is said to originate from the Kurubas.

The Ajapaveda, or Aja (meaning goat or sheep), is considered the root of all Vedas, where "Aja" also refers to knowledge. The Kurubas believe that their wisdom is unparalleled, with Aries being the source of knowledge, occupying the first position in the zodiac cycle.

In Northern India, the Kurubas are also known as Pal or Bhagel, which translates to strength like a lion. The Kurubas identify themselves as Palakshatriyas, Rajaputs, Maratha Kshatriyas, and Thakurs, with similar gotras (lineages) to Kshatriyas and Vaishyas. Historically, the Kurubas opposed Mughal rule and controlled vast forested regions, as recorded by Dr. Made Gowda.

Scholars trace the term **Dhanga**r (another name for Kurubas) to the 1st century AD, with "Dhang" meaning hill. The Kurubas, thus, were known for their connection to mountainous regions. Some scholars also suggest that the word Kurupa evolved into Kuruba over time, possibly from the name 'Kurupa Anna', meaning mountain.

There are legends connecting the Kurubas to Lord Shiva, who is said to have called shepherds Kaurubas, which might have later become Kuruba. These legends also credit the Kurubas with founding the first kingdoms in India, establishing small settlements that would eventually grow into towns and cities. The Kurubas were instrumental in starting various professions governance, soldiering, farming, teaching, and more.

In South India, particularly during the Pallava dynasty, the Kurubas, also referred to as Kurumbajans, were powerful. Tamil scholar Pingalam calls them Kurunila Mannar, meaning small kings. Historians like Lakkappagowda have also linked the Vijayanagara kings, such as Harihara and Bukkaraya, and the Kadambas to the Kuruba community, further cementing their role as rulers and builders of early Indian civilization.

In conclusion, the Kurubas were not merely a community of herdsmen but were deeply spiritual, wise, and instrumental in shaping the early social, political, and cultural fabric of India. Their legacy as rulers, scholars, and protectors of nature continues to be recognized in historical texts and cultural traditions.

Shambhajoshi's research provides a detailed account of the Kuruba people, describing their vast presence from the southern Kaveri basin to the confluence of the Narmada and Godavari rivers in central India. He concluded that the Kurubas were a pre-Aryan people, emphasizing their deep roots in Indian history, even referring to them as 'Kandamilas'. Other scholars, like Heurat and H. Wilson, have also associated the Vijayanagara kings with Kuruba heritage. In *Vidyaranya Kalagyana* and *Keladi Nripavijayam*, the Kurubas are referenced as "Kuruvamsa Prasutija," signifying their connection to royal lineages.

S. Krishnaswami Iyengar, in his book *The Sources of Vijayanagara*, further delved into the genealogy of the Vijayanagara kings, describing them as members of the Sangam clan, specifically the brothers Harihara and Bukka. He also referred to them as Kurumbalayara, firmly connecting them to the Kuruba community. The name "Bukka" itself is said to refer to those who slaughter goats and sheep, strengthening the link between the Kuruba profession of shepherding and the rulers of Vijayanagara.

Despite written records attempting to claim these royal figures for other groups, Pujarappa's narrative reinforces the belief that history belongs to those who lived it, and not simply those who wrote about it.

The word  Kuru, meaning height or mountain, further defines the Kurubas as a tribe residing in the hills. This connection is supported by ancient Tamil poetry, which refers to the Kurubas as Maleyaru, meaning those who live in high places. In Tamil Nadu, the Kurubas are known as Kurumba Idaiyar, and in Telugu, they are referred to as Kuruba or Kuruma.

In South Dravidian languages, "Ku" or "Koo" signifies a hill, and "Kuru" refers to mounds or small hills. This etymological link further solidifies the Kurubas as a people closely tied to hilly and elevated landscapes, where they relied on goats and sheep for sustenance. According to Bishop Caldwell, the term Kurumba originates from Kannada rather than Tamil, signifying the deep cultural ties between the Kurubas and the Kannada speaking regions.

The Halumat folk tradition reinforces this by stating, "Kulavilla Gotravilla Kurubane Adige Falakano is human," meaning the Kuruba identity transcends specific castes or gotras. It is a reflection of their deep connection to the land and their unique cultural practices.

The Puranic tradition, while often mythological, offers a symbolic origin story for the Kuruba community. The tale of Muddappa and Muddavva's four children Adigonda, Anantagonda, Siddappagonda, and Padmagonda provides insight into their ancestral roots. The youngest son, Padmagonda, while seemingly aimless, is divinely tasked with caring for cattle and lambs, which he accomplishes through mystical means. His eventual success in shepherding, after a series of miraculous events involving Shiva's intervention, symbolizes the Kurubas' historical role as shepherds and their unique relationship with the divine.

This narrative draws a profound connection between the Kurubas' spiritual beliefs, their occupation, and their historical significance. Their culture is deeply tied to their environment living in hills, shepherding sheep and goats, and embracing both the spiritual and material worlds. The mix of folklore, historical documentation, and etymology illustrates the resilience and cultural pride of the Kuruba people, whose identity has withstood centuries of change and adaptation.

The narrative you're crafting delves deeply into the origins, history, and cultural significance of the Kuruba people, highlighting their roots as Dravidian people. According to lineage scientists like Dr Hadan and other authorities, the 'Kurubas', or 'Kurkh' people, are Dravidians who migrated to the plains of Chota Nagpur. This aligns with Dr. Hadan's assertion that Kurubas are of full-blooded Dravidian descent, a view echoed by scholars like Geti.

The Kurubas are described as a group that originally came from the Carnatic region, eventually settling in Bihar along the people's reach extended geographically from the Kaveri River to the Ganges and from the Nilgiris to the Rajmahal Hills, showcasing their widespread influence.

Scholars like Gesto Overteen have also referred to the Kurubas as the oldest living people in India, characterizing them as indigenous and nomadic. The Kuruba lifestyle was highly dependent on the availability of water and pasture for their animals, which led them to wander extensively. Their settlements were often called Hatti or Rappalu in Telugu, denoting their nomadic nature.

Dr. Sunithakumar Chatterjee, who studied the Dravidian people, suggested that the Harappa and Mohenjo daro civilizations were Dravidian. The discovery of Linga mudras and Pashupati (Shiva) idols at these sites suggests that the Kurubas were likely participants in this ancient civilization. This ties their history to one of the most significant early cultures in the Indian subcontinent.

Geographically, the Kurubas spread across regions like Nashik, the Rajmahal Hills, and the Chotanagpur basin. Scholars like

Anthony and Dr. Grierson identified them as Karuka and Dhanagara in these regions. Over time, Kuruba groups such as Kadukurubalu, Zenukurubalu, Andekurubalu, and Mullakurubalu migrated to various parts of India in search of food and better living conditions.

W. Elliott, another notable scholar, referred to the Kurubas as one of the most important social elements of South India, likening them to the Dhangars of Maratha and North India. This connection highlights their widespread cultural and societal impact across regions.

The Kurubas, with their tradition of wearing bangles and utilizing natural resources like cotton for various needs, have maintained their cultural identity while also adapting to changes. The discussion of fluctuations and separations within the Kuruba community hints at potential divisions, but the call to unity especially during gatherings like the Gudikatla ceremony reiterates the importance of solidarity among the Kuruba people.

Vosikeri's observation, as he listens to Junjappa's speech, reflects his realization of the rich and often overlooked history of the Kuruba people, especially within the Telugu speaking community. The historical depth shared by Junjappa resonates strongly with the audience, as evidenced by their enthusiastic engagement, selfies, and newfound pride in their cultural identity.

The Gudikatla ceremony itself serves as a powerful reminder of the strength in numbers and the unity of the Kuruba people. It instills in them a sense of pride, belonging, and self-confidence, as they witness the gathering of so many people united by their shared heritage. Vosikeri, like many others, feels both a sense of awe at their collective strength and a deep sense of responsibility to preserve and celebrate their culture.

This story beautifully blends historical research, cultural identity, and the modern-day reflections of the Kuruba people, as they reconnect with their roots and find strength in their unity. The message is clear: by embracing their past, the Kuruba people can confidently shape their future.

The atmosphere at the event was electric, and everyone praised the hard work of the organizers who managed to bring so many people together. The sheer size of the crowd was overwhelming. Vosikerappa, seeing the massive gathering, couldn't help but reflect on where all these people had been over the years. He thought, Have I distanced myself from them, or have they been out of reach all this time?

Deeply moved by the stories and songs he had heard, especially the tale of Beerappa, Vosikerappa wrote down the narratives with great interest. The lectures about Gudikatlu wrapped up late at night, and the announcement on the microphone reminded everyone that the next program would start early in the morning. Vosikerappa and his family spent the night at the junior college ground, where they slept under the open sky. As he lay there, Vosikerappa was filled with a sense of awe at the rich history of the Kuruba clan. He marveled at the awareness and pride that had emerged within their community. I am working on my project at the perfect time, he thought, feeling fortunate to document this cultural revival.

Before dawn, Pujarappas were already busy. They removed the withered flowers from the previous day and replaced them with fresh ones to redecorate their temples. As the morning broke, Gudikatla owners from Kalyandurgam Road transported breakfast to the temple in their tractors. People admired the silver and gold offerings, discussing the wealth that was being displayed.

Among the crowd, whispers spread about the amount of money that had been collected. Some people from other castes muttered in disbelief, noting how many were contributing to the offerings. These people aren't foolish; they know how to keep their wealth safe, one person remarked. It was rumored that large sums were being brought to Anantapur for usury, and the townspeople gossiped about the influence these Kuruba leaders had in the region.

Different castes, meanwhile, were building their own complexes in town, and the discussion about interest rates and financial dealings continued. Despite the crowd, people from various castes came to see the spectacle at the temple, curious about the grandeur of the Gudikatlu. They made their way past Saptagiri Circle and the clock tower, finally arriving at the PTC ground, where all the gods from the Gudikats were assembled in a grand circle, each deity seated on a carpet. The sight of all the temples gathered together felt like a reunion of long lost family members. It was a rare sight, with so much to take in that two eyes didn't seem enough.

As Vosikerappa and Nagamma took in the scene, Nagamma suddenly stood up, intrigued by something. What's caught your attention? Vosikerappa asked.

"It's such a strange decoration; that's why I stood," Nagamma replied, her eyes fixed on a specific display. She turned to Pujarappa, who stood nearby, and asked,

"What is the name of this lord,

"**Muptellappa** Ammayya"

Which village?

Pujarappa responded, "It's Norpala Ayya."

Nagamma was fascinated by the unique arrangement and asked, "Why is this decoration different from the others? It looks special."

Pujarappa explained, "This lord is indeed decorated in a special way. The horses were set up first, with their saddles, and then thirty-three holes were made."

Nagamma, curious about the symbolism, asked, "Why is this pit shaped like this? I haven't seen anything like it before."

Pujarappa smiled and replied, "Amma, this is how the lord is adorned. We use thirty-three as a symbolic number, representing the word Sarvamu (everything). That's why even today, people in the villages say, 'I should do thirty-three,' meaning they should do everything. It's a way of symbolizing completeness and the totality of all things."

Vosikerappa listened closely, realizing that the deeper he delved into the history and culture of his community, the more he discovered layers of meaning in their traditions. The number thirty three, just like the intricate decorations and rituals, represented something far more profound an acknowledgment of the wholeness and unity that the Kuruba people strived for.

The story continued with deep reflections on the traditions and the cultural dynamics surrounding the temple. The Gudikatlu priest's remark about the shepherd searching for the lost sheep and the joy that follows upon finding it was a symbolic reference that resonated across many faiths, especially among Christians. However, the priest hinted at something deeper, perhaps a more profound connection between the Kuruba community and their spiritual practices.

Nagamma, intrigued by the conversation, found reason in what the priest said.

The discussion then shifted to the historical struggles of the temple. It was revealed that during the colonial era of Tadimarri, the temple was taken over, and a Brahmin priest was appointed, sidelining the Kuruba priesthood. The colonists would pray to the god for their needs, and when their wishes were fulfilled, they took control of the temple. This sparked a fierce battle, with the Kurubas fighting to reclaim their sacred space. Even after the Kurubas won back the temple, the Boyapujars (another group) tried to hold influence over it for a long time. Through all of this, the Kurubas remained vigilant, as political leaders attempted to encroach on the temple's significance for their own power.

Nagamma, curious about other castes worshipping the god, asked if it was a common practice. Pujarappa explained that, locally, many castes, including Kapollu, Eedigawala, and Boyel, worship the same god. These castes would come to the huts of Itikulapalleiya, and others would even come to **Chana Gudikatla**. The inclusivity of the Kuruba faith was evident in how it welcomed everyone, reinforcing the principle that their religion was about unity rather than division. The religious people of the community were more concerned with fostering peace and togetherness, rather than creating divisions among castes.

Nagamma then noticed something peculiar about the horse decoration a bridle and eyes on its back. Pujarappa explained the symbolism, saying that the horse represented the mind, and the bridle was a reminder of the *Arishadvargas* the six enemies of the mind (lust, anger, greed, attachment, pride, and jealousy). If the mind, like a horse, is not controlled, it could lead to one's downfall. Nagamma, curious to know more, was about to ask another question when Vosikeri gently intervened, telling her to give Pujarappa a break from her inquisitive nature.

Nagamma smiled and agreed, staying silent for a while.

As they observed the scene around them, the devotion of the people became more apparent. People were gathering not out of political influence or promises of gifts, but out of genuine reverence and devotion. There were no politicians making speeches, no media trying to create a spectacle, and no invitations sent out to lure people in. The masses had come purely because of their faith in the god, a stark contrast to modern gatherings driven by material incentives.

Vosikeri was awestruck by the scene unfolding before him. It was as if the people had emerged from the forests, like a tidal wave of humanity flooding the landscape. He looked around and saw people everywhere: in the fields, by the food stalls, in buses, in tractors, on motorbikes, on foot an endless stream of people, so many that the very ground beneath them seemed to shake. The sheer magnitude of the gathering was overwhelming, with no patch of land left untouched by the crowd.

This spectacle of devotion made Vosikeri reflect on the power of collective consciousness, how such a large group of people could come together in unity, driven by their shared faith and culture. This was more than just a festival; it was a testament to the enduring spirit of the Kuruba people, their resilience, and their unwavering dedication to their traditions.

Just then, a sound like a distant rumble echoed through the air, growing louder with every second. The people gathered at the event instinctively looked up at the sky, their attention caught by the increasing noise. The wind picked up, swirling dust and debris through the crowd. Some people whispered that it was an airplane, but those who knew better quickly corrected them. "It's not a plane, it's a helicopter," someone said with certainty.

As the helicopter descended, excitement rippled through the crowd. "Ayyoappa, it's Siddaramaiah!" someone exclaimed, referring to the Chief Minister of Karnataka. The speculation grew louder, with people discussing whether it really could be him. Some remembered the last time he came to the Kurubolla meeting in Anantapur five years ago. "It must be him," they said, their voices buzzing with anticipation.

Others, like he will not come, seemed more cynical. "What difference does it make if he comes? Even if there's conflict among us, it's like a mother and child fighting nothing serious. He'll be here to make an appearance, nothing more," one person commented. Another voice in the crowd chimed in, saying, "There's never been much decorum among the Kurubollu anyway."

As the helicopter hovered lower, the crowd erupted in excitement. The machine circled the PTC ground, just high enough that the man guiding it could almost reach out and touch it. The cheers and whistles from the crowd grew louder as the helicopter began to descend. People shielded their faces from the dust being kicked up by the powerful winds, their eyes watering from the particles swirling around them. The smell of earth and something unfamiliar, almost like a storm or a wild force, filled the air.

Then, something extraordinary happened. From the sky, a shower of flowers rained down over the temples set up in a circular arrangement on the PTC ground. It was as if the heavens had opened up, blessing the deities below with a cascade of petals. The crowd's joyful uproar grew as they watched in awe. The gods on the ground were bathed in a forest of flowers, a scene so surreal that it felt like a glimpse of paradise.

As the flowers continued to fall, some people murmured in disbelief, "Has this ever happened before? Our gods are being honored in a way that's never been done flowers from a helicopter! This must be a first in history." Vosikeri stood watching, mesmerized by the spectacle unfolding before him. It was unlike anything he had ever witnessed. He felt a sense of pride welling up inside him, a realization that the Kurubas were far more dynamic, developed, and powerful than he had ever imagined. The realization that so many Kurubas had become politicians, leaders, and well-educated members of society filled him with awe.

However, despite the celebration and the overwhelming sense of unity, Vosikerappa couldn't help but feel a pang of disconnection. He thought about how little contact he'd had with the people of Anantapur district over the years. Though he was a Kuruba, he had never attended meetings or celebrated the cultural milestones like Kanakadasa's days or Krantiveera Sangolli Rayanna's anniversaries. He avoided social gatherings that tied him to his caste, not out of disdain, but because he feared the obligations that came with it. If I meet people, he thought, I'll have to spend time with them, which means money, tea, coffee, and dinners  things I don't want to bother with.

Nagamma, his wife, had always been vocal about their need to avoid unnecessary social ties. We don't need this, she would often say. We dont need connections to caste, relatives, or society outside our home. We don't need anyone."

Yet deep down, Vosikeri longed to be part of the community. He enjoyed speaking with people, laughing and sharing moments. His honesty was his strength, and he had never relied on anyone else's money. No one could cheat him because he was always clear and upright in his dealings. But still, he held himself back, thinking, May be it's better this way.

Despite his reservations, Vosikeri couldn't help but feel a surge of caste pride rising within him as he watched the massive gathering. For so long, he had avoided identifying too strongly with caste, seeing it as a divisive system. But now, seeing the Kurubas come together like this, he felt something stir inside him. He began to wonder if perhaps he had been wrong all along maybe there was value in these connections. The strength of the community was undeniable and seeing them all together in such force made him question his earlier choices.

For a brief moment, Vosikeri entertained thoughts of holding a meeting, a grand event that could bring the Kurubas even closer. He imagined warning them of external threats foreign religions attacking their faith, much like how fundamentalists often spoke of their battles in far off lands. It was a fleeting thought, one that he quickly dismissed, chalking it up to the mischievous whispers of the devil. No, that's not the answer, he reminded himself. He wasn't here to stir conflict, but to observe, understand, and reconnect with the heritage he had distanced himself from for so long.

Vosikeri's mind was racing faster than the flowers falling from the helicopter. While the people around him were mesmerized by the spectacle of the floral downpour, his thoughts were swirling with doubts and reflections. No one knows me here, he thought. Despite the grandeur of the event and the respect being shown to the gods, Vosikeri felt invisible, as if his presence didn't matter in the larger scheme of things.

The helicopter continued to circle above, showering flowers for more than an hour. The gods, now covered in a blanket of blossoms, seemed to be offering silent thanks to the heavens. But amidst this divine spectacle, Vosikeri's inner world was in turmoil. The wind picked up again, and the dust returned, forcing people to cover their eyes. Some waved at the helicopter, while others muttered about the pilot, wondering if it was someone from their community. "Even for a rent could fly that helicopter if paid enough," someone joked. The question of caste and occupation seemed irrelevant to them now pilots, gods, and the people all felt intertwined in this moment.

Vosikeri watched as the managers were showered with praise, their egos swelling with each compliment. The celebration around him was filled with laughter and drunken joy. "I've never seen anything like this," some of the older people marveled, impressed by the scale of the event. Vosikeri, though tempted to speak his mind, held back. I am a professor at the university, he reminded himself, *and these people, they're just caught up in the moment.

In Tirupati, where he lived, few people knew him as a professor. He liked it that way. Even his neighbors and relatives weren't fully aware of his work. There was no need for anyone to know he valued his privacy and the peace that came with it. Why should anyone here know about me? he thought. His marriage, his career, all of it seemed distant from this crowd and the lives of those around him.

As Vosikeri was lost in thought, a man wearing a tie arrived in a car and walked into the PTC ground. The youth greeted him with respect: "Namaskaram, sir! Namaskaram, sir!" Curious whispers spread through the crowd some asked who this man was, while others assumed he must be an important official. Vosikeri's younger brother, Eranna, recognized the man instantly. "Lay Yadagiri Sir Ra!" Eranna exclaimed, remembering Ayyappa, a respected figure in the family.

Yadagiri had always been a responsible man, dedicated to his family and the community. He had secured a good government job after his degree and lived comfortably in Anantapur. He helped many people, often taking the time to guide his relatives, ensuring their children received proper education. Ayyappa even took months off work to coach students, providing them with the knowledge and skills they needed to succeed. Eranna spoke highly of him, admiring his selflessness and dedication.

As Eranna praised Yadagiri, Vosikerappa's thoughts turned inward once again. They think Yadagiri is doing great work, shaping lives, helping people,he mused. And yet here I am, with my own accomplishments, feeling like I don't measure up.

The distance between Vosikeri and his family seemed to widen in his mind. His detachment from the celebrations, from the community, and even from his own parents weighed on him. Despite all he had achieved, he felt as though he was standing apart, not part of the tapestry of their shared life and history.

When Vosikerappa and Ramanji arrived at Dadulurappa's house, they explained they needed help with a Kannada book. Dadulurappa quickly called Narayanappa's son Nagasheshu, who was studying in Bengaluru.

Nagasheshu replied, "I'm in Hyderabad for three months, but after that, I can help with the book. Give them my number."

Dadulurappa shared the number with Vosikerappa and Ramanji, and they thanked him for his assistance.

Vosikerappa woke up early and left for Tirupati. He traveled to Mushtikovela, where people gave him a lift by cart, and from there, he reached the NS Gate and then Dharmavaram, boarding a train at half past ten. Upon arriving home in Tirupati, he and his wife Nagamma quarreled briefly before returning to their usual routines.

The next day, Vosikerappa received a call from Rasani Venkatramaiah, a retired Telugu lecturer from Venkateswara University. Venkatramaiah had heard about Vosikerappa's research on Kuruba history and Beerappa and called to discuss it.

"Hello, Sir, I'm Vosikerappa, working as an Anthropology lecturer at SV University."

"Ah, yes. I've retired after teaching at a degree college. What can I do for you?" Venkatramaiah replied.

"I've been living in Tirupati for years, but we've never met. I'm writing a book on Kuruba history and Beerappa. I need some help."

"That's great," Venkatramaiah said. "I had always wanted to write about Kurubas myself, but I'm glad you're doing it."

"I'd appreciate any help or information you have," Vosikerappa added. "It's part of a UGC project I've been working on for six years."

Venkatramaiah recommended some sources. "There are good stories from Telangana about Beerappa, especially from Late Oggu Sathaiah and now his grandson Dr Ostad Oggu Ravi. If you talk to them, you'll get more detailed stories, particularly about Mallanna."

He also suggested Vosikerappa speak with Bandinarayana Swamy, a novelist, and Maddaiah, a historian from Kurnool. Venkatramaiah shared their phone numbers.

Later that day, Vosikerappa called Maddaiah, who agreed to meet him the next day in Kurnool. That night, Vosikerappa took a bus to Kurnool, lost in thought about the significance of Kuruba history. The next morning, he reached Kurnool and made his way to Maddaiah's house.

Maddaiah greeted him warmly, and over coffee, they discussed the project.

"What's driving you to write this history?" Maddaiah asked.

"I've studied hard my whole life, but aside from supporting my family, I feel my education hasn't contributed much to society. Now, I want to complete this UGC project on Beerappa before I retire."

Maddaiah nodded. "That's noble, but remember, research needs depth. People don't always understand the layers behind myths. For instance, the story of Padmagonda and the snake pit is symbolic. It speaks of ancient rituals and fertility. There's science and meaning behind these traditions."

Vosikerappa, inspired, realized how much more there was to uncover. He expressed how seeing the Gudikatla celebrations had ignited a sense of responsibility in him to document his culture's unique history.

"Sir, I want to give back to my community through this project. After witnessing the Gudikatla celebrations, I feel like I'm doing this for something bigger than myself."

Maddaiah smiled, understanding the passion behind Vosikerappa's work, and offered his support in whatever way he could.

Vosikerappa listened carefully to Maddaiah's words, nodding along with the sharp observations about caste, politics, and history. Maddaiah spoke with conviction, discussing the harsh realities of power and caste dynamics.

"Yes, who really cares?" Maddaiah began. "People get married, leave their homes, and move on. Even the politicians from our own caste, they pretend to represent us, but what have they done for our race? People of other castes are doing research and helping their communities financially. What do our politicians do? Once in power, they become part of a special class politicians, who are no longer tied to caste. They act like they are above it, just for votes."

Maddaiah leaned forward, "The same goes for other castes Reddy's, Kamma's, Madiga's they all have poor people, yet politicians act like their caste is free from suffering. The truth is, politicians are a class of their own, and they don't care about the people, even if they pretend to."

He paused, "But tell me, what do you want from me? If you're doing research, tell me openly. People don't do anything nowadays without expecting something in return."

Vosikerappa quickly clarified, "No sir, I'm not doing this with expectations. Yes, the UGC project gives me a grant, but I don't want to just write for the sake of it. I want to go deeper, to uncover the cultural truths. I've lived in my own little world all these years, and now I want to share the real stories facts, not just surface level histories."

Maddaiah nodded thoughtfully. "That's a good intention. But remember, when you study a caste, you have to study everything highs, lows, everything. Some people boast about their caste, saying, 'We are the people of this land,' but what do they gain from ruling? You need to study cultural life, not just claim heroism."

He continued, "History is written by those who put in the effort. Whoever created it, wrote it. Why make someone else a hero in the history you write? You need to approach this with scientific scrutiny check if the facts are credible. Evidence is what matters. Without it, people just make baseless claims, and unfortunately, people believe them because it's easier to accept myths than question them."

Maddaiah's tone turned a bit somber, "You know, soldiers who fight for kings are often forgotten. History only remembers the rulers, not the soldiers who sacrificed their lives. The same is true for those guarding our country today no one talks about them. It's all politics. Everything is."

"You're right, sir," Vosikerappa agreed. "But doesn't that mean the effect of these writings, of this research, is even more necessary? Modern society may have advanced, but superstitions and false beliefs still dominate. They affect everything, and we have to show the truth."

Maddaiah leaned back in his chair, considering Vosikerappa's words. "Yes, superstitions still have a strong hold on people. That's why what you're doing is important but only if you do it right. Don't fall into the trap of glorifying myths. Be honest with the evidence, and you'll write something that matters."

Vosikerappa knew then that his research would need to challenge long held beliefs, but he was ready to take that step, knowing that people like Maddaiah were guiding him along the way.

Maddaiah began by questioning the repetition of ancient stories, "How long have we been recycling the same tales from scriptures? Why not think of something new? We must critically evaluate what's passed down to us."

Vosikerappa agreed, listening intently as Maddaiah explained, "Cultural history isn't about recovering the past, but about examining our present to find what's been lost. The common people, their traditions, and customs this is where true history lies."

The conversation shifted to the Kuruba caste, with Vosikerappa asking, "When did our caste originate, and why are we called Kurubolu?"

"Caste wasn't immediate," Maddaiah said. "Man came first, and as survival skills developed, so did caste distinctions. But the Kurubas, early herders, played a vital role in organizing society."

When asked about Beerappa, Maddaiah emphasized, "Beerappa  is more than a deity. He represents the spirit of the Kurubas a protector, a unifier. He's a symbol of Shiva, embodying values that have guided the Kuruba people for centuries."

He added, "Beerappa 's story ties the Kurubas to a much larger history, from ancient civilizations like the Sumerians to the Indus Valley. His legacy is one of resilience and unity."

Vosikerappa realized the significance of his research. Beerappa wasn't just a cultural hero he was a figure who connected the Kurubas to a profound historical and spiritual legacy.

Vosikerappa and Maddaiah discussed the origins of civilizations and how the Kuruba culture fits into that history. Maddaiah linked the Sumerian civilization to the Kurubas, mentioning that both worshiped shepherd kings, with parallels to the Akkadians and Mesopotamians. He highlighted that Dumuzi, a shepherd king from Sumerian culture, rose to prominence amidst persecution, much like how Beerappa symbolizes strength and resilience for the Kurubas.

Maddaiah continued, noting that just as Sumerians revered kings as gods, the Kurubas similarly elevate Beerappa to divine status. "Beerappa isn't just a deity," he emphasized. "He's a cultural and historical figure who represents the shepherds' way of life and their survival against oppression."

The conversation touched on migration and how different cultures, like the Aryans, may have integrated into existing civilizations rather than conquering them. Maddaiah argued, "We shouldn't fixate on the Aryans displacing us. It's more important to focus on how we, the Kurubas, preserved our identity and culture through figures like Beerappa ."

The discussion closed with Maddaiah pointing out that civilizations, from Sumer to the Indus Valley, revolved around cattle rulers, and worship evolved around the forces responsible for life and fertility. "Beerappa, as a god of the Kurubas, reflects this ancient heritage. His significance goes beyond religion he's the embodiment of the Kuruba people's history and struggle."

Vosikeri, in his discussion with Maddaiah, explored the origin of divinity in human culture. Maddaiah explained that the concept of gods arose as humans sought to understand and control the powerful natural forces around them. Fear of the elements and their impact on life led to the creation of rituals and worship practices.

He emphasized that the earliest forms of worship among pastoralist cultures, like the Kurubas, were centered on life and fertility symbols such as the Linga (phallus) and Yoni (vagina). These symbols were directly tied to the idea of creation and birth, reflecting the Kurubas deep connection to nature and livestock. Traces of these worship practices, including Shishna Puja (phallic worship), have been found in ancient civilizations like Harappa and Mohenjo Daro, showing the global prevalence of such rituals.

Maddaiah mentioned that even in modern day Japan and China, similar fertility festivals and rituals still exist, underscoring the universality of these practices. He linked this ancient form of worship to the later deification of figures like Lord Shiva, who, in his naked form, represents the primal forces of creation and destruction.

The conversation also touched on the transformation of these rituals as civilizations grew. As new cultures emerged, the worship of fire, nature, and fertility evolved into more sophisticated religious systems. Maddaiah noted that the term "Arya," often misunderstood as a race or civilization, simply means "noble" in Sanskrit and does not signify a specific group or origin.

In conclusion, the discussion highlighted that Beerappa, for the Kurubas, is not just a deity but a reflection of their ancient pastoral roots. The worship of fertility, creation, and nature forms the backbone of the Kuruba cultural identity, which evolved alongside humanity's understanding of divinity.

Vosikeri's conversation with Maddaiah deepens his understanding of Beerappa as a cultural and historical figure. Maddaiah explains that the term "Indra" in ancient scriptures is not a specific god but refers to a king or emperor, a term synonymous with those who have no control over their senses. The word "hero" in ancient cultures, including Greek, was used to describe individuals with exceptional bravery, skill, or valor.

Beerappa, much like the Sumerian hero Dumuzi, represents a historical and cultural icon. Maddaiah draws parallels between Beerappa and other ancient figures, including those from Sumerian civilization, highlighting the trident like weapon both Beerappa and Dumuzi wielded, symbolizing their role as shepherds and protectors. He also connects Beerappa 's worship to the broader tradition of hero worship, evident in different cultures, such as the Sumerians, where kings and heroes were often deified after their death.

The concept of Veeragallu stones commemorating heroes who sacrificed their lives for the community is significant in understanding Beerappa 's legacy. These stones, found near Shiva temples, indicate that Kurubas were not only worshipers of Shiva but also warriors who defended their communities. Maddaiah emphasizes that Veeragallu and Mastigallu (stones commemorating women who practiced self-immolation) are unique to Kurubas, reinforcing the idea that they were a community born for battle and sacrifice.

Beerappa 's worship, according to Maddaiah, is ancient, dating back to the 4th century, with records of him being worshiped as early as the Bandaru culture. The cultural hero Beerappa symbolizes not only spiritual devotion but also the resilience and bravery of the Kuruba community. Through the story of Beerappa, Vosikeri learns that his community's heritage is deeply rooted in the traditions of heroism, sacrifice, and a connection to nature, all of which shaped the cultural identity of the Kurubas.

Vosikeri's exploration of Beerappa 's history brings him into contact with Maddaiah, who shares deep insights about the ancient heritage of the Kuruba community. Beerappa is highlighted as an ancient cultural hero, with roots tracing back to times when shepherds played pivotal roles in society. Maddaiah explains that Beerappa is often seen as a historical figure who mirrors the worship of pastoral deities like Dumuzi from Sumerian civilization, emphasizing the ancient connection between shepherding and divinity.

Maddaiah elaborates on Beerappa 's antiquity, connecting him to the customs and practices of the Kuruba people, who revered him as a protector and warrior. The conversation touches on the fact that many Kuruba traditions, including the worship of Beerappa, predate the Aryans and are deeply ingrained in the cultural history of India. Beerappa is not merely a folk hero but a symbol of the community's resilience and their ancient connection to the land, animals, and spirituality.

Vosikeri, intrigued by the historical depth and the connections Maddaiah draws between Beerappa and global ancient practices like Linga and Shishna worship, realizes that Beerappa is not just a local god but part of a larger, universal human history. Maddaiah's insights about the hero stones (Veeragallu) further solidify Beerappa 's status as a hero who sacrificed for the community, a theme prevalent across various ancient cultures.

As Vosikeri continues his journey of uncovering Beerappa 's historical significance, he is inspired to bring this rich cultural heritage into his research, recognizing the importance of preserving these stories for future generations.

Vosikeri's journey into uncovering the history of Beerappa deepens as he explores the historical and cultural roots of the Kuruba community. Through his encounters with scholars like Maddaiah, Chandrakanta Bizzarige, and Siddappameti, he discovers that Beerappa is not just a folk deity, but a historical and cultural icon tied to ancient pastoral traditions, similar to those seen in Sumerian and other early civilizations. Beerappa is revealed to be a protector and a symbol of resilience for the Kuruba people, tracing back to a time when shepherding and animal husbandry were central to human survival and societal organization.

Maddaiah emphasizes that Beerappa 's legacy predates Aryan influences and that he holds a significant place in Indian history as a leader of the pastoral communities. These communities, known for their sacrifices and heroism, are embodied in the Veeragallu (hero stones), which commemorate their bravery. Vosikeri also learns that the rituals, practices, and beliefs associated with Beerappa have universal parallels, as seen in the worship of similar figures in other ancient cultures.

Nagasheshu, Vosikeri's companion in this exploration, is equally fascinated by the depth of Beerappa s legacy. They travel to meet Siddappameti, a folk singer who preserves Beerappa 's history through song. Despite facing challenges with language barriers and cultural differences, they realize that Beerappas narrative is crucial to preserving the cultural identity of the Kuruba people.

As Vosikeri prepares to document these findings, he faces personal struggles at home with his wife, Nagamma, who questions the value of his research. However, Vosikeri remains determined to fulfill his goal, inspired by the rich cultural history of Beerappa and the Kurubas. His commitment to preserving this heritage for future generations becomes his driving force, seeing it as a way to honor the past while contributing to the collective identity of his community.

## Hampiyatra

That night, Vosikeri called and spoke to Nagasheshu, asking when they would leave for Hampi.

"We should go this week," said Nagasheshu. "I've finished my research submission, and there won't be a problem until the viva."

"Good, talk to Hallikere today," Vosikeri replied.

"I just did.  he said us to come anytime. He'll be available."

"Then let's get ready."

The next day, Vosikeri and Nagamma had a discussion. Nagamma's father, Kittappa, had come over to talk sense into her.

Kittappa, not understanding Vosikeri's commitment to his research, warned him, "There are many people who study race and religion but end up wasting their time. You have a good life don't throw it away."

"No, Mama, I'm doing this with the conviction that it will bring respect to our name," Vosikeri explained, standing his ground.

Later, Vosikeri spoke to his children over video call. They were encouraging, wishing him all the best. Even Nagamma, though hesitant, gave him her quiet support.

The next morning, Vosikeri called Nagasheshu, telling him he had booked a train from Dharmavaram for the next day. From there, the two set out for Hampi.

Upon reaching Hampi, they arrived at the university's library, where they brushed and washed their faces. Vosikeri marveled at the size of the library, commenting on how strong the universities in Karnataka seemed to be. Then, they contacted Hallikere, who directed them to the Hallumata Mahapeetam.

After a quick breakfast, they went to meet Hallikere. He showed them the vast collection of books and palmistry texts. After lunch, the trio strolled through the expansive university grounds, which resembled a forest. Vosikeri, seeing fewer students, asked why.

"Most students stay in nearby Hampi or Hospet. The forest scares them off," Hallikere explained.

The day ended with Hallikere arranging a guest house for them, which Kempanna, the in charge, led them to. The guest house was secluded, with only a watchman present. Kempanna warned them about bears and snakes, making them uneasy. The night was restless, especially when a cobra slithered nearby, adding to their discomfort.

The next day, Hallikere provided both a set of 50 cassettes and a thick book titled "Janapada *Halumata Mahakavya*", a thousand-page work filled with ancient songs and stories. Vosikeri, realizing the challenge of translating the Kannada text into Telugu, sought Nagasheshu's help. After receiving the materials, they made their way back to Tirupati to begin the task.

Once settled in Tirupati, they dove into the work. The book started with the story of Beerappa 's ancestors and the many challenges they faced. The text, rich in folklore and history, was narrated through songs, revealing the deep cultural significance of Beerappa in the Kuruba community.

In their quiet moments, the duo reflected on their journey to Hampi, the knowledge they had gained, and the immense task ahead. Despite the obstacles, Vosikeri felt a renewed sense of purpose, ready to bring the story of Beerappa to life for future generations.

# Janpadha Dreams

Shiva and Parvati descended from Kailasam to Bhuloka (earth) for a summer retreat, or bejaresinde. As they explored the natural beauty around them, they were delighted to see the animals, birds, hills, valleys, and the features of the land. The sound of the mountains, the beauty of the valleys, and the rhythm of pebbles in the rivers filled them with excitement. Parvati, in awe of the scenery, remarked to Lord Shiva that this place was even more beautiful than they were.

"Look at that land in the middle of the water," Parvati pointed out. "It's full of green trees. Two eyes aren't enough to take in all the beauty of this place."

Shiva, with wisdom, responded, "Yes, all the beauty of the goddess is found on earth, but people are dying for trivial reasons. They give up the lives we gave them without experiencing the beauty of this world. It's because they lack the intelligence to truly see and experience it."

Parvati, deep in thought, decided that they should also spend some time enjoying the beauty of Bhuloka. Shiva, agreeing with her, suggested that they stay for a while.

As they explored the land further, Shiva remarked, "People often look at these rivers and think there is something special in our world. It's the unknown that fascinates them."

Then, he pointed towards the forest and said, "Parvati, look at these forests! Breathe in the wonderful smells that fill the air."

Parvati, overwhelmed by the delightful fragrances, tried not to exhale, wanting to savor them.

Shiva chuckled, "The scents that have enchanted you so much can only be perceived in the measure that we need."

Parvati, curious, asked, "Natha, where do these fragrances come from?"

Shiva gestured towards the deer in the distance, "Look at those deer, grazing and wagging their tails."

"Yes, the deer," Parvati responded. "But what about this sweet aroma?"

Shiva explained, "Those deer are no ordinary animals, Devi. They are special. The musk deer produce a sweet-smelling substance, yet they wander across the valley searching for the very scent that comes from their own bodies. Hunters search for this smell and take their lives for it."

Parvati, struck by the irony, said, "Isn't it fascinating, Swami, that these deer search for what they already possess? Isn't this true for humans as well? They wander the earth, seeking something that lies within them all along."

Shiva smiled and said, "Yes, Devi, that's exactly the point."

Parvati, feeling playful, suggested, "Swami, why don't we turn into musk deer for a while and enjoy these beauties ourselves?"

Shiva agreed, and both of them transformed into deer. However, Parvati soon realized that the fragrances they once enjoyed as gods were no longer present in their new form.

Shiva reminded her, "Devi, the scents you are searching for come from within, just like the musk deer who don't realize that the aroma is produced by themselves."

Parvati, concerned, noticed Shiva playfully jumping and twirling around. She worried he might injure himself, especially as he darted between the trees. Shiva was in high spirits, but his antics eventually led to an accident. There was a loud sound, and Parvati's heart raced as she saw Shiva with a broken horn and an injured head.

She rushed to him, gently placing her hand over the wound and said, "Oh, Natha, what have you done? You turned entertainment into tragedy."

The antler from Shiva's deer form had fallen, and blood was flowing from the injury. Shiva, touching the wound, realized that he had been struck hard. He picked up the fallen antler and decided that it should remain on earth.

Parvati, worried, pleaded, "Swami, look what has happened in just one day! If you stay here, you will never return to Kailasam."

Shiva, in his divine wisdom, said, "Devi, if I am to stay, I shall stay here in the form of this antler."

Parvati then declared, "If this antler is buried in the ground, it will transform into a Shivalinga."

She asked Shiva to ensure that the antler would be buried and turned into a divine symbol.

After the incident, Parvati urged Shiva, "Let's return to Kailasam before more such accidents happen."

As they prepared to leave, they both marveled at the beauty around them. Parvati pointed to the river in the distance and said, "Look, Swami, can you hear the sound of the river flowing? Doesn't it sound like the angels themselves are singing?"

Shiva, amused, responded, "Yes, Devi, the sound is enchanting. This mountain is known as Kailasaparvatam, the place where I resided before we were married."

Parvati, with a playful tone, replied, "But Swami, you are quite mischievous. What is the name of this river?"

Shiva, curious himself, asked, "What is it, Devi?"

Parvati smiled and said, "This is the Indus River, which originates high above sea level in Mount Kailash in Tibet. Flowing through Ladakh and past the Jaskar Lake, it turns south near Nanga Parvat and eventually joins the Arabian Sea. The Indus River crosses only a small portion of the land known as Ajanavarsha."

Shiva asked, "Ajanavarsha? What does that mean?"

Parvati explained, "Swami, Ajanavarsha was the ancient name for India."

Shiva, intrigued, listened as Parvati continued, "The tributaries of the Indus include the Jhelum, Ravi, and Sutlej rivers. Before the Vedic period, the Indus was known as Vurnavati. In what is now Himachal Pradesh, the land between the Chenab and Ravi rivers was called Vornamandi."

Shiva asked, "What about Parushti?"

Parvati replied, "Parushti refers to wool. It was called that because wool was traded along this river."

Shiva nodded, appreciating the beauty around them. "Yes, Devi, the shepherds are truly the children of nature. Wherever they go, there is greenery."

Parvati, curious again, asked, "Swami, why do they live in these tents?"

Shiva explained, "There was a time when man tamed animals. Until then, man hunted freely, but eventually, he learned to feel compassion for these creatures. He began rearing sheep, goats, and cattle, and as he did, he set up tents like these. It's a natural way of life, close to nature."

Parvati agreed, "Yes, Swami, living close to nature brings a special kind of joy."

With that, they reached Kailasa once again, their hearts full of the beauty and lessons they had experienced on earth.

## "Flock of Shiveshwara"

He still could not forget the dream that came to Shiveshwar at night. He is following the sheep with concentration. Meshanadu is situated on a high place on Narakanda Hill. Among the dogs near Shiveshwar, Sarlakukka is doing something with its forepaws. As if something has hit her leg, she is squinting. It stood there looking at it repeatedly.

Sheep and goats keep moving forward. Shivesvara moved a little forward and looked back. All the dogs came, but only one stood there. Calling did not come, whistled and did not come. It will slow down. No matter how much Shiveshwar called, when the dog did not come, he himself ran back to see.

She is sitting looking at the antler of a deer that fell down before her legs. Thinking that this is a weapon for hunting, he took it in his hand. Endappa saw this. He was surprised to see the half broken deer horn. He took the horn in his hand and turned it.

He turned again and again to see if this is what I dreamed of in the night, if it was something like this or if it was a deer horn. Taking the handkerchief tied on his head in his hand, he lowered it and sat on it, turning the horn and looking at it. What is this antelope that came to me in my dream at night? But he is muttering whether I am in the place where my lord walked. He thinks he can't believe if this is art or real.

In the meantime, the cows that were going away were frightened by the noise and scattered in different directions. He barked loudly and barked at the dogs. The wolf is dragging the Ram by the throat. The dogs were gone before they were gone. Running and panting, he came to Gorlamanda. He is worried that it would have been better if I had gone back.

He is walking  along sheeps while worrying. He is walking holding an antler in his hand. He stared at the horn again, thinking that it was not lost. Is this branch in the night dream? This is the image of Lord Shiva

He thought it was coming. What I dreamed of at night has now appeared in this form. He thought again for a long time whether this was real or an art.

He thinks that what Parvati said to my lord is true, why should we bury it in this earth like a good dream? So he buries that horn in the ground like a tree in the north next to the 'Lahela' valley. For that, he squeezes the milk of black goats every day when he takes the sheep to graze.

He also shared this with his fellow shepherds around when he was shepherding at night. They were very surprised and said that we will also come to the place tomorrow and take care of it. As expected, the herd was driven towards 'Lahela'. Seeing the deer's horn, thinking that it is God, the sheep and goats drink milk and pour it on the deer's horn.

The cowherds are milking every time they come to the pastures. As the days passed by, the devotees came in large numbers to spread the news. A small canopy was also placed on the deer's horn so that my lord would be in the sun. The matter has spread to surrounding villages such as Meshanadu and Chandragiri.

## Charity of Lord Tripureshwara

Tripureshwara, the wealthiest shepherd in Meshanadu, was known for his immense flocks and his seven children, all involved in tending the sheep. One day, tragedy struck Mayavva's son, Singamayya, who lost all his sheep when a fire destroyed the barn in the middle of the night. Mayavva, in desperation, sought help from the community and eventually turned to Tripureshwara. Moved by her plight, Tripureshwara, known for his generosity, donated some of his sheep to help her recover, embodying the principle that those with wealth should aid those in need.

Tripureshwara was revered in Meshanadu and Chandragiri for his acts of charity. His devotion extended to his belief in the divine, especially in the sacred antlers of Lord Tripureshwar, which were worshipped in the Lahela region. He longed to have seven daughters and seven brothers, and in devotion, promised to offer the finest rams of his flock if his wish was fulfilled.

As Tripureshwara and his family passed through the forests of Jamakanda one day, they decided to stop for lunch. Jamakanda, the forest's keeper, furiously confronted them, striking Tripureshwara for eating in "his" forest. Despite being attacked, Tripureshwara chose not to retaliate and left peacefully. However, the forest mysteriously began to wither soon after. The local villagers, attributing the curse to Jamakanda's mistreatment of Tripureshwara, urged him to apologize.

Jamakanda, filled with remorse, begged Tripureshwara for forgiveness. Tripureshwara, embodying mercy, forgave him but also advised him to show respect for shepherds in the future, as they were crucial for the prosperity of the land.

Years later, the same forest flourished again when Tripureshwara, his family, and their sheep returned to the area, reaffirming that the presence of shepherds brings fertility and abundance.

The cycle of conflict resurfaced when Shiveshwar, another devout shepherd, drove his flock through the Jamakanda forest, and the sheep accidentally grazed in Jamakanda's garden. In anger, Jamakanda attacked Shiveshwar, but the forest soon began to die once more. Shiveshwar, respecting the lesson learned by Tripureshwara, left without escalating the conflict.

**Tripureshwara's Battle with Konasura and the Rescue of His Daughters**

Tripureshwara, known for his strength and kindness, valued his daughters more than anything. One day, while tending to his sheep near **Vurnavati**, he was ambushed by Konasura, a notorious thief who lived in the huts around Manyakhet. Konasura's gaze fell upon

Tripureshwara's flock and, more disturbingly, on his seven daughters.

The dogs guarding the sheep barked and tried to ward off the attackers, but Konasura silenced them with a powerful blow. Tripureshwara, ever the protector, quickly intervened. The confrontation escalated as Konasura's men outnumbered Tripureshwara, and in the chaos, they began to harass his daughters.

Desperately fighting back, Tripureshwara managed to grab Konasura by the throat, frightening the thief and forcing him to let go of the girls. But Konasura struck back, and Tripureshwara called out in a booming voice for his daughters to flee. His seven daughters ran to the Poornavathi River, where they jumped into the water in a desperate attempt to escape.

As they were being swept away by the current, Muddamma, the youngest of the seven, cried out in terror, her voice carrying through the wind. Shiveshwar, who happened to be near the river, heard her cries and rushed to their aid. Without hesitation, he dove into the river, saving Muddamma first and then the others, pulling them to safety one by one.

Despite being rescued, the daughters, particularly Muddamma, were distraught. They questioned why they had been saved when they had resigned themselves to their fate in the river. Yet, Shiveshwar's timely intervention and their survival left a profound impression on them, particularly Muddamma, who could not shake the feeling that her life had been spared for a greater purpose.

In her distress, Mayava asked Tripureshwara for help. Moved by her suffering, Lord Tripureshwara gave her some sheep as a gift. He believed that if someone lacked wealth or was in trouble, the best way to help was to give what one had.

This gesture of generosity wasn't uncommon for Tripureshwara. Whenever anyone in the region had a need, he provided them with resources from his wealth. As a result, the people of Meshanadu and Chandragiri held a deep devotion to him.

One day, Tripureshwara, along with his herd of sheep, visited the place where the sacred antelope horn had been planted in the Lahela area. Devotees had been worshipping the horn, and Tripureshwara wanted to join them. He believed that the antler held great power, and he made a vow in his heart: if his desire to have seven daughters and seven brothers in one family was fulfilled, he would offer the best of his sheep as a sacrifice to the horn.

The local shepherds and herdsmen were all competing with each other to worship the sacred deer's horn. They discussed constructing a shelter for the horn, as it was vulnerable to the elements, especially during rainstorms. They chopped down large trees nearby and used the timber to build mud walls and lay firewood horizontally to create a large canopy over the site.

Once the shelter was built, the community began debating who should be appointed as the priest for this newly constructed temple. Since Shiveshwar had been the first to worship there, it was decided that he would continue the worship and lead the temple rituals. Because the cowherds, or Kurubals, had built the temple, it was named Pashu Pati, which means "Lord of the Animals."

The Pasupatalayam was located on the route from Lahela to Tenkanad, with Jamakanda forest lying in between. One day, Tripureshwara, along with Manda, was traveling towards Tenkanad. As it was midday, they decided to rest and have their meal in the forest on the Tenkanad Margam. While they were eating, Jamakanda appeared, furious at the sight of strangers eating in his forest. In a rage, he threw their food, and Tripureshwara fell to the ground.

Seeing Tripureshwara injured, his family—both his wives and children—immediately started arguing with Jamakanda, accusing him of trying to dominate the forest. However, Tripureshwara prevented them from retaliating. He believed that it was his own fault for entering the forest without permission and accepted that he had no right to strike back. He left Jamakanda unharmed and departed from the forest.

In the following days, however, the entire Jamakanda forest mysteriously dried up. Jamakanda, realizing that the forest's decline coincided with his quarrel with Tripureshwara, began to feel guilt and remorse. The local people also blamed Jamakanda, saying that the curse of harming Tripureshwara was the cause of the forest's demise. With their advice, Jamakanda approached Tripureshwara, begging for forgiveness.

Tripureshwara, being compassionate, forgave Jamakanda's unintentional mistake and told him that it was all in the past. Jamakanda, however, insisted on showing his repentance through actions. Tripureshwara, reluctant at first, agreed to visit the forest again with his family, as Jamakanda had requested.

The following day, Tripureshwara and his family went to the forest. Almost miraculously, within a few years, the forest began to flourish again, turning green and full of life. Jamakanda, grateful and relieved, thanked Tripureshwara for restoring the forest's vitality. Tripureshwara then advised him to never harm or blame shepherds, for wherever they went, they brought abundance and prosperity.

Some time later, Shiveshwara was grazing his sheep near the same Jamakanda forest. Feeling thirsty, he ventured into the forest to drink water. While he was away, the sheep wandered into Jamakanda's garden and began grazing there. Jamakanda, furious, found Shiveshwara and beat him for trespassing. Shiveshwara, though he resisted at first, eventually decided it was better to retreat rather than escalate the conflict. He left the forest, and once again, within a few years, the forest began to wither.

Jamakanda, realizing his error, went to Tripureshwara and sought advice. Tripureshwara reminded him of the previous incident and urged him to respect the shepherds, for they were under divine protection.

In the region around Manyakhet, there lived a powerful thief named Konasura. His reputation for theft was widespread, and he seized whatever he set his eyes on. One afternoon, Konasura spotted Tripureshwara's flock of sheep grazing on a high hill near the Vurnavati River. With his band of men, Konasura attacked the herd.

The dogs guarding the sheep barked loudly, but Konasura struck them down. The dogs scattered, whimpering as they ran away. Tripureshwara rushed to defend his sheep, but Konasura and his men outnumbered him. In the ensuing fight, they began to assault Tripureshwara's daughters and wives. The girls screamed for help, but Konasura's men continued their assault, harassing the women and attempting to steal both them and the sheep.

Seeing this, Tripureshwara grabbed Konasura by the throat in a fit of rage. His strength momentarily frightened Konasura and his men, causing them to release the girls. But before long, Konasura struck Tripureshwara with a heavy blow. As the fight escalated, Tripureshwara's daughters, terrified, fled towards the river.

Desperate and screaming for help, the seven girls were swept away by the river's strong current. The youngest, Muddamma, cried out louder than the rest as they were all carried downstream.

At that moment, Shiveshwara, who had been grazing his flock nearby, heard the girls' cries. He rushed to the river, where he saw the girls struggling against the current. Without hesitation, he dove in and rescued Muddamma first, followed by the others, pulling them from the water one by one.

When the girls were safely ashore, they expressed mixed emotions. "Why did you save us?" they asked, "We were destined to be lost. Why did you intervene?"

Tripureshwara was deeply grateful for Shiveshwara's bravery. As a token of appreciation, he arranged for Muddamma to marry Shiveshwara, offering some of his sheep as part of the marriage tradition. According to the custom, the name of the groom was whispered three times into the ear of the sheep, and the marriage ceremony was conducted as per the shepherding traditions of Meshanadu.

However, the other six daughters, feeling indebted to Shiveshwara for saving their lives, insisted on marrying him as well. Although Shiveshwara only wanted to marry Muddamma, he was eventually persuaded to marry all seven.

After the marriages, Shiveshwara's responsibilities increased, and his attention to the temple, where he once worshipped, began to wane. Devotees continued to worship from outside the sanctum, but a rule was established that only Shiveshwara could enter the temple to perform the rituals.

## Muddamma's Prophecy and a New Dilemma

Muddamma, the first of Shiveshwar's wives, soon became pregnant. This news brought hope and joy to the household, but also unease. One evening, a mysterious soothsayer named Sodi arrived at their tent. She had a reputation for accurately predicting the fate of families through birth horoscopes. Muddamma, curious and slightly apprehensive, allowed Sodi to read her future.

Sodi sat quietly for a few moments, holding Muddamma's hand under a blanket. Then, with a grave expression, she opened her eyes and spoke.

"Lord Shiva's presence is strong within your family, but there is a curse upon you, Muddamma. Though you will bear a child, this child will not live long. You will lose it before it even has the chance to be born. This is Parvati's curse."

Muddamma was stricken with shock, her heart sinking like a stone. The soothsayer's words struck deep, and she felt the weight of divine wrath upon her. Sodi went on, explaining that Muddamma had, unknowingly, incurred the displeasure of the goddess Parvati. Even Shiveshwar's negligence of his temple duties had contributed to the curse.

# The Consequence of Neglecting the Gods

Muddamma's dread intensified. She hadn't realized how deeply her family's fate was intertwined with the gods' will. She wept silently, believing that the curse was a result of the actions she had unknowingly taken and her husband's abandonment of his divine responsibilities.

Desperate to change their fate, Muddamma sought Shiveshwar's counsel. Together, they decided that Shiveshwar must return to his duties at the temple to appease the gods. Shiveshwar, realizing the gravity of his neglect, resumed his daily prayers and rituals, returning to the temple to offer milk and flowers to Lord Shiva. He vowed never again to stray from his path of devotion.

Though Shiveshwar's prayers were fervent, the fear of losing the unborn child lingered heavily in the air. Parvati's curse loomed over the household, and they were left wondering whether their renewed devotion would be enough to lift the curse before it was too late.

# Beerappa A Historian, Culturalist

Beerappa believed that God exists because events happened as they did. He often said that Lord Shiva would tell her this. Shiveshwar, however, was deeply hurt and began to feel depressed, wondering why such hardships were happening to him. Despite this, he resumed his regular worship at the temple, where he used to pray with deep devotion.

While sitting in the puja, he questioned, "Why are you putting us through all this suffering, even though we have worshipped you with such sincerity?" Yet, Shiveshwar firmly believed that everything is the will of God.

After some time, Shiveshwar and his wife were blessed with a son. They remembered the curse from Goddess Parvati, who had told Sodamma to abandon the newborn and leave. Though Sodamma was reluctant to leave the child, she feared that if she stayed, something bad would happen to him.

Shiveshwar, however, reassured her, saying, "It doesn't matter where we are, as long as the child is safe." He suggested to Muddamma that they head into the forest and, if they came across anyone, they could give the child away. If not, they would leave him in the bushes.

Suddenly, an idea struck him. He remembered Bettappa, a man he knew very well, known for his kind heart. Bettappa was a devout man who visited the temple every day. Shiveshwar decided to ask Bettappa secretly to take care of their child.

Muddamma agreed. Early the next morning, they placed the child in the trees near a muddy puddle, where sheep would drink water. Bettappa, learning about the curse, agreed to help.

However, Bettappa's wife, Guttakka refused,  did not accept the idea of taking child as this may bring bad luck to them.

Shiveshwar continued his journey through the forest, laying all his burdens on Lord Shiva. Muddamma, overwhelmed by the pain of leaving her child behind, was inconsolable. She lay down on leaves, refusing to move or touch anything, crying out, "How sinful I must be, leaving a life behind. It would have been better if the waters had taken me too." As she placed the child on the ground, his legs and arms trembled, and he smiled. She looked at him and thought, "How cute you are, and I made you an orphan before you could even call me 'mom.'" She cursed God repeatedly, asking why she had been put through such agony.

Shiveshwar, seeing Muddamma in this state, forcibly pulled her away, saying, "We must leave before anyone sees us." The entire group was in tears. They left the child behind, trusting that Bettappa would come to take care of him.

Shiveshwar and his companions, who tended to a herd of sheep, moved through the forest, setting up tents wherever night fell and moving on at dawn. They continued this way for a long time, tending to the sheep. As time passed, Shiveshwar couldn't stop thinking about the child, and Muddamma struggled to keep up. Weakened, tired, and hungry, they fed on whatever they could find in the hills fruits, leaves, mushrooms, honey, and cheese milk.

One day, they pitched a tent in the valley of Kodgad. One of the sheep was feeding her lamb, and the women stood by, watching. The group spent the day grazing the sheep, tending to the herd, and seeking shelter from the rain as it began to pour. It was as if something mysterious had come over the sea. The voice of Lord Shiveshwar could be heard clearly from a distance, his calls echoing through the hills, urging them to climb higher.

The sound of thunder and flashes of lightning made it difficult to see anything clearly. Strong winds uprooted massive trees, and the sheep scattered in confusion. Their cries were drowned in the chaos, and even those nearby couldn't see each other's faces in the heavy downpour. In an instant, it felt as though a flood had surged, and the rain was so intense that the hills were awash with torrents of water.

Amidst the screams and the storm, they thought to themselves, "Wherever he may be, we must find him, even if it's for the last time." Nature's call was unstoppable, a force that united everything. That call brought a sense of calm amidst the chaos an equanimous and harmonious call, one that they all heard together. In that moment, nature gathered them all, as if to take them under its care.

# Kongudweep

No one knows who got lost, who survived, or who perished. Tellare had fallen into the middle of a land area surrounded by water. Muddamma slowly opened her eyes, unsure if what she was seeing was real or if she was still alive. As she looked around, all she could see was water. She searched for everyone, but no one was in sight. She blamed God, begging for a second chance, the pain of loss overwhelming her, and the sorrow was indescribable.

She questioned why God would spare her life, feeling there must be some reason behind it. She could barely remember anything beyond being swept away by the torrential rains. The realization of her survival brought her to tears, as she hadn't expected to live through such an ordeal. Her tears mixed with the surrounding water.

Meanwhile, the child, abandoned by his mother, cried out in loneliness. Gukkapatti, either hungry or grieving for his mother, wept bitterly, separated by fate and the will of the gods.

The cry of the child reached the ears of Adivanna, a wanderer who heard the sound and found the baby. He picked up the child, though he himself was lost in the wilderness. Adivanna was like a monk of modern times, doing no specific work, and the people around him admired him for his mystical knowledge of rattavidya (some form of esoteric knowledge). The surrounding Rappalas (perhaps a group of people) revered him as a god, believing he had the power to foretell events.

As soon as Adivanna held the child, the crying ceased. He took the baby to the village and sought to discover who the child belonged to. He considered the situation incredible and told everyone that no harm should come to this child.  He was also known as Barama.

Adivanna had no family, no home, and no set place to live. He didn't ask anyone for anything. He simply carried the child with him wherever he went. Occasionally, he would ask shepherds for milk and feed the child.

Seeing Adivanna's difficulty, a man named Lingayya offered his help. Lingayya told Adivanna, "Don't trouble yourself by asking for milk every day. Bring the child to where my sheep are, and I will milk them for him." Sometimes, Adivanna would leave the child with Lingayya for a while. Lingayya took great care to involve the child in his daily tasks, and whatever Adivanna ate, he shared with the child. They slept wherever they could find shelter. There was no clear home or family structure, but everyone believed that if Adivanna was raising the child, no harm could come to him.

The child, Barama, grew strong day by day, like a mountain, under the care of Lingayya and the nurturing hand of Bettappa.

Meshanadu includes Bettappa and his wife, Guttakka. When the child reached an age where he could play, a special ritual was performed, where the name "Tagaru" was whispered into the child's ears as part of an Aries ritual. Guttakka was known for her strong will, and humans found her difficult to deal with. Above all, she cherished her baby girl, who brought joy into their lives.

# The Story of Bettappa, Barama, and the Shepherds

Bettappa had a younger sister named Suramma, and all three of them, Bettappa, his wife Guttakka, and Suramma, lived by shearing sheep. Bettappa had a strong devotion to Lord Shiva, and every morning he would rise early and offer white flowers to the deity.

However, in Manyakheta, two asuras (demons) named Konasura and Mundasura were causing trouble for the local shepherds. These demons would steal sheep, and if caught, the shepherds would stone them to death. The shepherds lived in constant fear as the demons feasted on stolen sheep, growing stronger and more powerful.

Many shepherds from Meshanadu, Chandragiri, and the surrounding areas fled, unable to withstand the terror. Some settled along the banks of the Varnavati River, and others ended up in Kandahar, either because the land favored them or they couldn't cross the large rivers. A few others settled in what is now Balochistan, as the land there was suitable for sheep herding.

Bettappa and Lingaiah had many sheep in Meshanadu. They built fences to protect their sheep, but Lingaiah and his wife Gauri had no children. The people in the village gossiped about them, calling them cursed for being childless. Whenever Gauri or Lingaiah came across the sheep, people would hurl insults at them, believing their misfortune was contagious.

Due to the constant humiliation, Lingaiah began to view Gauri as unlucky because they had no children, and he wouldn't allow her near the sheep for fear that bad luck would strike. Gauri remained isolated, and Lingaiah blamed her for everything, even saying that the sheep would get sick if she approached them.

Meanwhile, the shepherds were slow to graze their sheep during the day because they were terrified of Konasura, who would sneak out from the bushes and pounce on them.

t is difficult for the sheep to eat bananas, but when the sheep come near the tents, he worries that something might happen to Gauri. If anything happens to her, he thinks it will be because of

Shanimunda's curse, and he fears the consequences. Even the people of Rappaal don't want to get involved in saving such ill-fated people.

Shepherds aren't slow, even during the day. There is always a fear that Konasura might emerge from the bushes and attack.

'Nagappa and Sangamma' make their living by collecting sheep skins and selling them in Chandragiri. In families like theirs, all the children born are girls. Children born on Sundays or during the Amavasya (new moon) or Kalo (a specific day) are immediately abandoned in the forest. These children, considered ill-fated, are left to die as soon as they are born.

While wandering in the forest, Adivanna encounters Sangamma. He decides to offer her some of the fruit he is eating. Sangamma believes that with the blessing of this fruit from Adivanna, she will give birth to a son this time. She is confident that Adivanna's gift will change her fate.

Nagappa, a sheep shearer, is overjoyed and starts preparing for the birth of his son. He imagines the days to come, thinking of all the things he will do with his son and what name he will give him. He dreams of raising the child and watching him grow strong.

But time moves swiftly, like the wind, and soon the moment of birth arrives. They had been waiting with great hope for the birth of a son, but once again, their hopes were dashed. A girl was born instead.

This time, however, the baby was different. All her organs were healthy, and she was born on a full moon, not on the dreaded new moon.

When Sangamma learned that she had given birth to another girl, she was devastated. She didn't even want to see the baby's face. Just as the village women had predicted, Sangamma cried out in frustration, ignoring the baby's cries. The child screamed, but no one paid attention to her.

Naganna knew about it and frowned. He thought to himself that these girls have caught him like a snake. He cursed himself, calling the situation "Shanimunda" (a curse), saying that seeing everyone as a girl has cursed him. Seeing the screaming baby, Naganna took the baby and threw it away in the forest without anyone noticing. He scolded Sangamma, saying that she too had fallen into a well or a pit. The baby, abandoned by Naganna, screamed in hunger. That very day, Lingaya, who was herding sheep near the tents of Chandragiri, heard the baby's cries.

He looked toward the bushes. It seemed like someone had just given birth, as the bloodstains were still fresh. He thought someone had abandoned the baby there. Thorns pricked the baby's skin, and he thought the child had been discarded like sheep's intestines. He picked up the baby and cleaned off the thorns that pierced its chin. He took the baby and presented it to Gauri.

"Whose child is this? It's so cute," Gauri thought. The child was bleeding from the thorns that had pierced it. Gauri took the baby under a tree and rolled it in the mud. To feed the baby, she milked the sheep, poured the milk into small flour baskets, and the hungry child drank with a strong gulp. The baby was deeply hungry and involved in the act of drinking. Screaming in pain earlier from hunger, the child stopped crying for a while after drinking the milk.

The childless couple received the baby as a blessing from Lord Shiva. They said, "This child is a gift from God to us. Everything is going well in our lives now that we have this child, as if Barama himself has entered us."

However, they feared that if they stayed near the tents, someone might discover their secret and take the baby away. Lingaya suggested that they shift to Kalgiri from Meshanadu. But Gauri was worried, saying, "Even if we move, they might still suspect us."

"No," Lingaya replied. "We'll tell everyone that our sheep have caught a disease called segadomma. That way, no one will get suspicious. If we lose this child, which we are so fortunate to have, the word 'children' will lose all meaning for us, and we will never be able to call ourselves parents."

"Fine, but I fear this baby might not live," Gauri said.

Lingaya retorted angrily, "Shanimunda! Why are you saying such inauspicious things? Speak good words and let the baby live!"

"Okay, I'll take care of the baby and the sheep. You go and shift the flocks to Kalgiri before evening," Gauri instructed.

In Kalgiri, a few houses already existed. They made noise and mingled with the people there. Lingaya told the flocks that their sheep had caught scabies and that they were moving away because of it. The people were afraid and stayed away from them. Barama slowly grew up, roaming the forest without any fear.

He turned into a lion, scaring wolves and jackals away. Whenever Barama saw them, he would chase after them. It was impossible to take a sheep when Barama was around. He ran at wind-like speed, never stopping until he caught a rabbit or an antelope. Lingaya cared for the sheep that gave milk like they were the apple of his eye. Barama feared nothing and could go anywhere alone. Seeing Barama's strength and courage, all the shepherds believed he was a hero capable of facing thieves.

Bettappa's younger sister, Suramma, was charitable like Tripureshwar. She helped anyone in trouble, believing that her devotion to God would bring blessings. Bettappa, however, disliked this. He was not fond of Suramma's charity, finding it annoying and unnecessary.

Adivanna was delighted by Barama's progress. No one knew where or when Adivanna would appear, but he always showed up when needed. Adivanna lived a life deep in the hills, surviving in the forests. He interacted with nature more than with humans, talking to stones, logs, trees, and stumps.

Lingaya had seven sheep that had been calving near his sheepfold, but he had trouble managing them. However, thanks to Adivanna's intervention and Barama's presence, the sheep gave milk plentifully. Lingaya began to believe that Barama was no ordinary man, but a god born to change their destiny.

Adivanna's connection with God was well-known across Meshanadu, Chandragiri, and Kalgiri. With Barama's bravery and heroism, Lingaya's flock of sheep grew tremendously.

As Barama grew older, Lingaya's flock became even more prosperous. Barama shared his desire to graze sheep as well. Lingaya, grateful for the boy's strength, gave him some sheep to tend to, saying, "With all this wealth, why should you wait to inherit it?"

Barama became the chief sheep shearer, ensuring that the flock was never in danger. He cared for puppies, dug deep holes to protect them, and made sure they grew healthy and strong. He believed that by adding special mixtures to the milk, the dogs would grow faster and be more capable of running.

Barama was always accompanied by his dogs, an axe in one hand, a hammer in the other, and a sickle tucked in his belt. He also wore a handkerchief on his head.

Bettappa, who had no children, would wake up early in the morning to collect flowers, patris, and garika grass. He would then offer these flowers in worship to the Shiva linga in the Pashupati temple.

Despite this, a conflict arose over who should perform the worship in the temple. Bettappa argued that anyone could perform the rituals, while the people of the village believed that only the descendants of Shiveshwara should perform the worship.

This disagreement led to a major conflict in Meshanadu, with the villagers insisting that the Shivlinga temple should be worshiped only by Shiveshwara's descendants. Bettappa, however, remained adamant about performing the worship himself.

The elders of the village, along with Adivanna, decided that the matter should be resolved with Lord Shiveshwara's guidance. When Adivanna spoke, Bettappa remained silent.

Thus, the differences between Bettappa and Barama over temple worship continued. When the people of the tents supported Barama, Bettappa found himself isolated.

Bettappa plotted to solve the issue by suggesting a marriage between Barama and Suramma. This would ensure peace between the families, and Bettappa hoped it would solidify his control over temple worship.  Barama agreed to the marriage but insisted on consulting Adivanna first. Adivanna and Lingaya both agreed, saying that the marriage should follow traditional customs.

Suramma and Barama got married, and the couple moved to an area called Chandragiri, where they lived together in a tent. Guttakka, Bettappa's wife, was secretly happy that Suramma would not have children and sent her root powder that would prevent childbirth.

The couple, trusting Guttakka's advice, drank the powder daily. They continued living happily, shearing sheep and growing their flock.

Guttakka's real intention was to make them childless.  Despite Guttakka's deceit, the newlyweds were content and continued their sheep shearing work.

# Mabbudevara Festival

Time passed quickly, and every five years, the Shunyamamasa Mabbudevara festival was celebrated. Bettappa believed it was time for this important ritual and wanted to invite his sister, Suramma, home for the occasion. He asked Guttakka for permission to invite Suramma, but Guttakka was against the idea. She said that since Shanimunda had left their home, she felt peaceful and didn't want Suramma, whom she considered unlucky, to return and disrupt their lives.

However, according to tradition, it was essential to have a daughter or sister present during special rituals like Mabbudevara. Without this, the festival wouldn't be complete. Bettappa felt it was wrong not to invite Suramma, so he sent a man to Chandragiri to bring her back.

The man arrived in Chandragiri and conveyed Bettappa's message to Suramma, inviting her for the Mabbudevara celebration. Suramma was hesitant and asked Barama why her brother was calling her after so long. Nevertheless, Barama encouraged her to go, saying it was a family tradition.

When Suramma returned to her brother's house, she was met with coldness. Bettappa, despite having invited her, didn't speak a word to her. Suramma, who had hoped for a warm reunion with her brother, was heartbroken by his indifference. She thought he might still care for her, but his silence deeply saddened her.

As time passed, Suramma and Barama's wealth and prosperity grew. The people around them began to recognize Suramma's greatness, and many encouraged her to become a mother. Suramma, still believing in her faith, told them that any blessings she had were due to Lord Shiva's grace.

Despite the challenges and Guttakka's efforts to prevent Suramma from bearing children, Suramma remained hopeful and devoted, believing that everything was in the hands of divine grace.

Some individuals made fun of Guttakka, saying she bore a bad omen, especially whenever they saw Suramma. When Suramma returned home, her brother didn't even acknowledge her or greet her. She wondered, "Why did he call me if he didn't care?"

That night, it was cloudy, and the preparations for the ceremony began. The front of the tent was cleaned, and powdered leaves from five types of trees were sprinkled around. Tangedu leaves were brought in and decorated with five kalapal flowers. There was a strict rule about the precise arrangement of the leaves and stones. Five red pebbles were placed, with three facing east and two facing the opposite direction. Two swords were placed on either side of the altar, named "Eerlu." Bettappa arrived, holding a black goat for the sacrifice.

There was fear in the air, as everyone knew the goat must not scream during the sacrifice if it did, something ominous would happen. Slowly, they caught the black goat and brought out a large machete wrapped in cloth to keep it out of sight.

At the Ratiposa place, the goat was examined. There must be no white spots on the body; it had to be entirely black. After confirming the goat was spotless, the person holding the machete faced east, murmuring something under his breath. The people there silently offered prayers to the sun, moon, and mother earth. Bettappa untied the cloth from the knife and prepared for the sacrifice.

Bettappa asked for permission to proceed, and when everyone gave their blessing, he raised the machete and swiftly struck the goat's neck. The head separated from the body, and the torso throbbed with the last signs of life as blood poured into a pot. The goat was skinned, and its entrails were divided into five parts, tied to the five pillars around the stone altar. The remaining meat was cooked for everyone, and the leftovers, including the bones and organs, were buried in a hole on the premises.

Suramma, along with the others, completed the Mabbudevara ceremony and left for her tents the next morning. Before departing, she told her brother that she was leaving, but he and his wife, Guttakka, ignored her. Some people began whispering, noticing how little attention was given to Suramma.

She walked away, crying and in deep pain, vowing never to return to this house. On her way back to Chandragiri, she thought to herself in agony, "Why did he call me if he was just going to humiliate me?" She pondered her place in her brother's life, feeling that if she were his child, perhaps he would care, but now it seemed her relationship with him was meaningless.

As Suramma journeyed through the trees, bushes, and forests, strange bird cries and eerie sounds echoed around her, heightening her sense of fear. Yet more than fear, the pain of being rejected by her family weighed heavily on her. She hadn't asked for anything no money, no inheritance, not even saffron. She wondered why her brother had called her only to disgrace her in front of others.

Just as she was lost in thought, a terrifying figure appeared Konasura, the demon, charged at her. Like a bear, he grabbed her tightly before she could even scream. In an instant, she was caught, unable to think or move. Suramma let out a desperate scream, calling out for help, but Konasura gagged her and continued to hold her down.

Barama, who had been herding sheep nearby, heard faint cries. Listening closely, he realized the screams were coming from his wife, Suramma. Without hesitation, he rushed toward her.

Meanwhile, Konasura was carrying Suramma on his shoulder, walking effortlessly through the forest as she struggled to free herself, kicking and hitting him. Barama, filled with fury, reached the scene with a machete in hand, determined to save his wife.

As Barama approached, Konasura threw him aside with a powerful blow, but Barama, undeterred, got up and fought back. The two engaged in a brutal struggle, with Barama grabbing Konasura by the hair and throwing him to the ground. Konasura retaliated by hitting Barama with a tree branch, but Barama stood his ground.

Suramma, still in Konasura's grasp, was terrified. She bit and clawed at the demon, but her efforts seemed in vain. However, Barama's strength and determination finally overpowered Konasura. He freed Suramma from the demon's hold and fought with all his might, driving the demon away.  In the end, Barama emerged victorious, rescuing Suramma from the clutches of Konasura. Both fear and pain mingled in Suramma's heart as she realized the depth of Barama's love and bravery. Together, they returned home, leaving the terrifying ordeal behind them.

Suramma trembled with fear as she clung tightly to Barama, recounting every detail of the terrifying incident that had happened to her. Sitting inside the tent, she explained how Konasura had attacked her, and Barama listened with growing anger. The thought of his wife being insulted and harmed was unbearable to him. He was filled with rage and was ready to storm out and destroy the village to avenge her.

But Suramma, sensing his fury, pleaded with him. "No, he is a friend of mine," she said softly. "But my brother's wellbeing is more important to me. Please don't kill him, Barama. Let's leave it here." She begged him not to seek revenge and to let the matter go.

In the midst of this emotional struggle, the sheep that they had been grazing were scattered. The flock, now lost, had been chased in different directions by wild wolves. Despite the chaos, some wolves managed to catch a few sheep and were resting happily after their hunt.

As Barama began to realize the severity of what could have happened to Suramma, he was more worried about the fate of his wife than the sheep. If he hadn't arrived in time, the loss would have been far greater than just a few sheep. He quickly gathered the remaining flock without much thought to what the wolves had taken. Suramma, too, helped in gathering the sheep. Barama didn't speak a word, and together, they herded the sheep until evening, returning them to the sheepfolds.

## Catching a Crocodile

Barama, although consumed with anger, decided to wait. He burned inside with the thought of the injustice that had befallen Suramma, but he chose to be patient, waiting for the right moment to act.

The next morning, as usual, Bettappa woke up and set out to collect flowers to worship Lord Shiva. He walked through the forest, but to his dismay, every tree he approached had already dropped its flowers to the ground. The local belief was that fallen flowers couldn't be used for worship, and Bettappa was deeply troubled. He wondered why this was happening and believed that only God had the answers to his troubles.

Bettappa decided to purify himself and fetch holy water. He took Sitala along and went to a nearby pond to collect water from the Ganga. As he stepped into the pond and bent down to fill the vessel, something strange happened he slipped and fell deeper into the water.

Suddenly, a crocodile emerged from the water, clamping its powerful jaws onto Bettappa. He struggled frantically but couldn't free himself from the beast's grip. Bettappa began to panic, shouting, "Save me! Save me! Lord Shiva, I pray to you every day, why won't you save me now?" He cried out in fear, realizing that he might not survive.

The crocodile dragged him further into the water, and Bettappa's desperate thoughts turned to prayer. He promised Lord Shiva, "If I escape this, I will offer you special flowers as part of my worship." But the struggle with the crocodile continued, the water churning with mud as the two fought.

Time passed, and the sheep remained in the paddocks longer than expected. When no one returned, Guttakka grew worried. Bettappa hadn't come back from his usual flower gathering. She looked around, wondering where he could have gone. Concerned, she called out, "Bettappa, Bettappa!" and began searching for him.

Guttakka was wandering, spinning in her thoughts, wondering what could have happened to Bettappa. Was he fetching water? Did something fall into the water, or had he been caught by something like a crocodile? Or maybe a snake had bitten him near the plants?

Meanwhile, Bettappa was still shouting for help, crying out, "Amma, amma!" Just as his strength was fading, Adivanna appeared at the scene. Seeing Bettappa struggling in the water, he quickly approached the lake. Bettappa, seeing Adivanna, gained a glimmer of hope and begged for protection. Adivanna, moving with urgency, slowly descended into the lake.

The crocodile had a tight grip on Bettappa, pulling him further into the water. But Adivanna, with his ax in hand, skillfully struck the crocodile, killing it. Despite the difficulty of the battle in the water, Adivanna managed to cut the beast and free Bettappa. As Adivanna tried to pull Bettappa out, he lifted him from the deep water, and finally, Bettappa emerged, like the moon being freed from the grip of Rahu.

Bettappa collapsed at the embankment, his body weakened, but alive. He woke up and immediately fell at Adivanna's feet in gratitude. Guttakka came running, screaming, and as she saw what had happened, she nearly fainted from shock. She was suffocating with fear and disbelief, wondering why such a terrible thing had happened. In her distress, she cursed, blaming Shanimunda for bringing such bad luck to their house, ever since Suramma had visited.

"I told you not to call her, but you didn't listen," she said. "This disaster happened because of my sister in law's visit."

Both Bettappa and Guttakka bowed down to Adivanna's feet, thanking him for saving Bettappa's life. Bettappa, who had faithfully worshipped Lord Shiva, was shaken to his core by the incident. Overcome with emotion, he said, "If I couldn't defeat the demon sent by God, I should have let the crocodile take my life today." Tears filled his eyes as he expressed his gratitude to Adivanna.

After the ordeal, both Bettappa and Guttakka hurried to check on the sheep. To their horror, they discovered that the wolves had attacked the flock. The sheep were scattered, and many had been killed by the wolves. The once full pastures now lay barren, and a tiger, full from its feast, sat watching the devastation from a distance. Bloodied wolves and jackals had joined the carnage, leaving destruction in their wake.

Guttakka, devastated by the sight, screamed, "Oh God, everything is gone, our very life support has been taken!" Shaking with grief, she ran toward the sheepfold and collapsed, sobbing uncontrollably. The wolves, with blood on their mouths, looked back one last time and slowly wandered away from the barn.

"We are cursed," she cried. "We are blamed by everyone for not having children, and now, we have nearly faced death by a crocodile. Disaster follows us every day." Bettappa, too, was consumed with worry. Why was this happening to them? They had lost almost everything, except for a few sheep that had managed to escape the wolves' attack. He cursed their fate, blaming Suramma's visit for bringing such calamity upon them.

Guttakka added, "Shanidevata has cursed our home; that's why all this is happening."

In their distress, Bettappa and Guttakka turned to Adivanna for guidance. "What is the reason for all these mishaps?" they asked. "What can we do to make things right again?"

Adivanna, after listening to their plight, advised them, "If you worship Lord Shiva with the leaves of *Enugulaguttavenakala A one leaf,* good things will begin to happen again. Your fortunes will return, and you will regain the wealth and comfort you once had."

Adivanna continued, "Actually, that day when I found you, I was lost in the forest. I had intended to go another way, but the path was different, and I was thirsty. Then I heard your cries and ran to help. Perhaps it was Lord Shiva, whom you worship, who sent me to you at that moment."

He ended with a prayer, encouraging them to worship with the Ondelaku leaves. "If you do this," he said, "good things will come your way, and your past wealth and happiness will return."

# A Single leaf

Bettappa set out to find the special leaf, A Single leaf , that Adivanna had told him about. Equipped with an axe, a stick, and a burji (a type of weapon), and carrying a torch to ward off wild animals, he began his journey toward Enugulagutta. Only Guttakka remained near the tents, anxiously awaiting his return.

Meanwhile, continued searching for the mystical Ondelaku. He scoured the hills, valleys, and vine covered trees, but no matter where he looked, he couldn't find the leaves he sought.

Barama, as usual, rose early to worship the Shivalinga near Meshanadu, and during the day, he sheared sheep. He now had a large flock, and along with his men, he tended the sheep during the day and guarded them through the night.

Bettappa, wandering through the forest in search of Ondelaku, lost his way. Whenever night fell, he would sleep wherever he could, always in fear, with no proper food or rest. He relied on the torch to keep wild animals at bay, but he felt utterly lost.

Eventually, he reached Gilgit, near the lower banks of the Vornavatina River. The people there seemed more civilized than those in Meshanadu, with better clothes and more advanced living. He noticed cows, bulls, horses, and even lambs, but they were not housed in the same simple enclosures he was used to. Instead, the animals were kept behind high mud walls. Bettappa learned that even the thieves in this place were less dangerous compared to those in Meshanadu. He merged into their society, observing how the locals made ropes from tree bark and used boats to transport goods across the river.

Everything seemed new and special to Bettappa. He even experienced a boat ride for the first time and was thrilled by it. He thought to himself, "I should do this too." With this inspiration, he began his own business, trading items across the river to the Indus basin.

# The Arrival of Mundasura:

One night, while Barama was resting after a long day of shearing sheep, trouble struck. His men were keeping watch, but suddenly the dogs began barking wildly, as if sensing danger. Barama woke up, alarmed, and grabbed his axe.

People began shouting that the dogs were under attack. Fear spread through the camp as Mundasura, the younger brother of Konasura, led a group of thieves from Manyakhet to attack Barama's flock of sheep. Knowing that Barama had killed his brother, Mundasura sought revenge. Armed with large bamboo sticks, the thieves flew over the walls of the sheepfold, ready to strike.

Barama engaged in a fierce battle with Mundasura, who attacked with the force of a monster. Though Barama fought valiantly, Mundasura's men overwhelmed him, and the two engaged in a brutal struggle. Barama was injured, but he managed to seriously wound Mundasura as well.

The chaos of the battle sent the sheep into a panic. Some sheep were killed by Mundasura's men, and others ran beyond the fields, bleating in terror. In the midst of the struggle, Barama and Mundasura continued to fight, while the rest of the thieves began slaughtering the sheep.

At that moment, the Rappa people from Chandragiri arrived to help. Armed with sticks, they joined the fight, and in the confusion of darkness, no one could tell who was hitting whom. It was like a battlefield, with both sides fighting fiercely.

Suramma, filled with worry for her husband, feared that something terrible would happen to Barama at the hands of the thieves. Despite the relentless struggles, Barama assured the people that they couldn't afford to abandon the sheep or their way of life out of fear.

# The Return of Bettappa:

Bettappa, who had been searching for Ondelaku, never found the leaves. He eventually returned to Meshanadu, forgetting about the sacred task. Instead, he resumed his business, which was thriving. But Guttakka and Suramma continued to suffer, burdened by endless problems and worries.

Barama shared with Suramma that Bettappa had now ventured into the linen business, and Barama himself wanted to shift focus to the sheep trade. Suramma agreed, and slowly, Barama expanded his business, starting with barter in surrounding villages. Eventually, his trade network reached as far as the Indus River, in what is today known as Baluchistan.

# Barama's Journey to Kongudweep

Barama learned from Adivanna that there were special flowers needed for worship, and he believed that these flowers could be found in a place called Kongudweep. Determined, Barama set out on horseback, armed with his axe and other tools, and crossed hills and valleys to reach this mystical place.

When he arrived, he found a land surrounded by water, with a small patch of earth in the middle. Barama was thrilled at the sight, and his joy knew no bounds. But as he explored the island, he came across an unexpected figure: a lone woman named Muddamma, living in isolation.

Muddamma's body was frail, her life a difficult one. She had been cursed by Goddess Parvati, and as Barama approached, she was struck by the thought that her long curse might finally be coming to an end. Barama, not knowing who she was, asked, "Who are you?"

Muddamma, filled with a mix of joy and sorrow, recognized that Barama was her long lost child, the very son she had abandoned in the bushes years ago. She couldn't believe her eyes her child had grown into a strong man. Overwhelmed with emotion, she was unsure how to reveal the truth.

Finally, through her tears, Muddamma confessed to Barama, "I am your mother."

Barama was stunned. He didn't know whether to feel joy or fear. He had come seeking a solution for his lack of children, and now, standing before him, was his own mother. The story of the curse and the abandonment came out in full, and Barama, though shocked, was filled with love and compassion for the mother he had never known.

Together, they embraced the truth of their past, and Barama's journey, which had begun in search of flowers for worship, became one of deep family reunion and healing.

Thus, the long curse of Goddess Parvati was lifted, and Barama's life took on new meaning, grounded in the love of family and the faith he had carried with him all his life.

Koravanji delivered the message to Bettappa, who had been plotting against his sister Suramma. Calling her to their home under the guise of caring for her, Bettappa had devised a plan to poison her unborn child without her knowledge, determined to rid himself of the threat he imagined the child posed.

Bettappa knew that Suramma might refuse to come if invited, so he thought of ways to trick her into asking for help, knowing she would be more likely to come under those circumstances. He and Guttakka discussed their plans before drifting off to sleep.

The next day, Bettappa decided to visit Chandragiri under the pretext of offering a gift. Guttakka wanted to accompany him but remembered the humiliation Bettappa had faced on Mabbudevara day, when he was cursed while worshiping the Shivalinga. She hesitated, reminding Bettappa of their family bond. "This is your own blood," she said. "If you refuse to go now, we might suffer more misfortunes later. You should go and make amends. Your younger sister will forget the past if you do. After all, what is there to be so proud of?"

Bettappa listened, and soon he arrived at Suramma's home. Suramma was overjoyed to see her brother. "How long has it been seeing you, Anna? Please, come inside," she said Welcomed warmly. Bettappa, playing the part of a caring brother, saibd, "I'm so happy to hear that you're going to be a mother. I've come to see you and want to spend some time with you on your birthday."

Suramma, though happy, declined to stay at her brother's house, saying, "No, brother, I'll stay here. I have too much to do at home taking care of the sheep and other things. My mother in law is also here. It's enough for me to see you." Bettappa, appearing disappointed but satisfied, returned home, hiding his true intentions.

Though Barama had been upset with Bettappa, he greeted him politely out of respect. Bettappa, wanting to avoid any suspicion, gave Suramma some seeds as a gift, pretending they were for her benefit. Suramma, unaware of his malice, gratefully accepted them. "Maybe these flowers are special and will help me," she thought.

However, Barama was suspicious. "How can we trust these seeds?" he asked Suramma. "This miscreant has caused us so much trouble, and now he's giving you seeds? How can we believe these will help?" Suramma, always optimistic, responded, "We've tried so many things, Barama. Maybe it's these flowers that will make the difference. Sometimes it's belief that makes things happen."

Despite his reservations, Barama relented and allowed Suramma to keep the seeds.

Back at home, Bettappa shared his dreams with Guttakka. He told her, "My sister spoke so lovingly to me, without hesitation. But I can't let this child be born it threatens everything." Together, they plotted to harm the unborn baby. Bettappa spent his time worshipping Lord Shiva, all while planning to kill Suramma's child.

One night, Suramma had a strange dream in which someone was calling her name. She awoke, unsettled, and went outside, thinking it might have been her brother. The next day, Bettappa arrived at Suramma's house with gifts: turmeric, saffron, cloths, and mutton. He called out to Suramma, who was surprised but happy to see her brother again. "Anna, it's been so long. How are you?" she asked, her heart lightened by his visit. Bettappa handed over the gifts, saying they were for her well being. But Suramma remembered her strange dream and felt uneasy. She wondered, "Why am I doubting my brother's intentions? What harm could come from gifts brought with love?" Yet, a nagging fear lingered in her mind.

Before eating the food her brother had brought, Suramma fed a piece of mutton to the dog outside. To her shock, the dog ate the meat and immediately died. Horrified, Suramma realized that something was terribly wrong. She suspected that the food had been poisoned without her brother's knowledge or perhaps with his full awareness.

In a panic, she recalled her dreams and wondered if they had been a warning. Suramma's trust in her brother was shattered, and she quickly sent him away, telling him that she would seek medical help from Manuri. She forgave him for what had happened but knew deep down that something darker was at play.   When Bettappa returned home and told Guttakka what had happened, they both despaired that their plan had failed. Suramma, still shaken, shared the events with Barama, explaining that the dog had died after eating the food Bettappa had brought. Barama was furious. "That evil man planned to kill our child! How can he be so cruel?"  Barama wanted to take action against Bettappa, but Suramma held him back, saying, "It's not worth it." However, Barama's anger simmered, knowing that Bettappa would stop at nothing.

As the time for Suramma's delivery  days approached, Bettappa became increasingly anxious, haunted by the words of Koravanji. His heart raced with fear, unable to sit still. He knew that his sister's child was destined for greatness, but he was consumed by jealousy and fear of what that child would mean for his own future. And so, the tension between Bettappa and Barama continued to grow, with Suramma caught in the middle, her unborn child the center of both hope and danger.

Various efforts were being made to harm Suramma's unborn child, and as part of this dark plan, Bettappa sent two midwives, known as *Sulagithas*, to assist with the delivery. The instructions were clear: as soon as the baby was born, they were to strangle the child immediately. Bettappa arranged for two butchers to accompany them, who were tasked with disposing of the body. He gave explicit orders that they were to cut off the baby's head and bring the trunk back to him, declaring that he would cook and eat the meat himself.

The *Sulagithas*, despite their fear and uncertainty, agreed to the horrific task and set off for Chandragiri, accompanied by the butchers. The night was dark, and their footsteps echoed as they walked through the wilderness towards Suramma's home. In the distance, the sounds of horses could be heard faintly, adding to the eerie atmosphere.

As the two Sulagithas approached Suramma's tent, fear gripped them. They stopped and sat by a mud wall, discussing their terrible plan and how they would kill the child. Meanwhile, the Rappa people, sensing something was wrong, heard the barking of the dogs and grew suspicious. The dogs were barking wildly, signaling that someone unfamiliar was near.

The midwives, scared and on edge, were caught by the Rappa people who were now alert. Holding firewood as weapons, they attacked the *Sulagitha*s without listening to their explanations. The women tried to say that they had come to assist with Suramma's childbirth, but the Rappa people were too suspicious of the strangers in the dark. They beat the midwives, and the dogs bit at their legs, arms, and bodies. The *Sulagithas* screamed, but the dogs wouldn't stop, even when the people tried to chase them away. The midwives, terrified, tried to escape, but the dogs attacked them relentlessly.

At the same time, inside the tent, Suramma was experiencing intense labor pains. Barama's mother had been brought to the house to help her, and the women of Rappala gathered around to offer support during the childbirth. Suramma, filled with pain, whispered prayers to Lord Pashupati, hoping for strength.

As the chaos unfolded outside, Suramma's mind focused on the birth. She was unaware of the deadly plot against her child, but her trust in the people around her and her devotion to the gods kept her spirits strong.

The Rappa people, unaware of the full extent of the conspiracy, managed to drive away the Sulagithas and butchers, leaving them wounded and unable to complete their sinister mission. Barama, standing guard near the entrance, was oblivious to the close call his family had just endured.

Inside the tent, the birth continued, and Suramma clung to hope as her thoughts focused on the wellbeing of her unborn child. All the while, she silently prayed for the safety of her family, unaware that they had just narrowly escaped a great danger.

# The Birth of Beerappa

During this pivotal time in Chandragiri, Suramma gave birth with the help of the women around her, and the baby was safely delivered. Nagasheshu, who had been meticulously writing Beerappa 's story, believed that Beerappa 's birth on the auspicious day of Shivratri was no coincidence. He felt a deep connection to this moment, having worked tirelessly without obstacles, as if everything had aligned perfectly for the birth of Beerappa .

Nagasheshu's dedicated assistant, Vosikeri, had been helping him throughout the process, often proofreading the story from the pages Nagasheshu had written. Every day, Vosikeri would take the draft and have it typed up by Thota Venkataswamy, who had a typewriter shop near the campus in Tirupati.

One evening, as Vosikeri read through the story, Nagamma joined him, expressing how proud they were of the work being done for Vosikeri's upcoming wedding. Yet, despite their happiness, there was a sadness that often surfaced, as Nagamma would question Vosikeri, saying, "Are you really one of us? Can you even complete your education properly? You and Nagasheshu are from the same caste, yet you're responsible for everything he does."

Vosikeri, however, took pride in his work. He felt that anything he contributed to would grow and flourish, and he often said, "Even if a single rupee is spent, it will yield great results." Vosikeri, though noticing that the meals sent from Nagamma's house for Nagasheshu were meager, yet he had advised Nagasheshu to eat at the university canteen instead.

One day, as Vosikeri and Nagasheshu were discussing their work, Nagasheshu's phone rang. It was Shivaratri, and the phone call came from  a person belonging to the Telugu Department at Bengaluru University. The clerk informed Nagasheshu that he needed to prepare for his viva within four days. Special meals and accommodations for the visiting experts were to be arranged. The phone call brought a sudden wave of stress for Nagasheshu, as he realized that providing meals and lodging in Bengaluru would cost a significant amount perhaps as much as 30,000 rupees.

Seeing the distress on Nagasheshu's face, Vosikeri understood the financial strain. Despite his own limited resources, Vosikeri quickly decided to offer his help. He quietly withdrew 30,000 rupees from his savings and placed it in Nagasheshu's pocket. Though Nagasheshu tried to refuse, Vosikeri insisted, saying, "This is for our community, for the success of our people." Vosikeri's act of kindness transformed Nagasheshu's mood, and his face shone with relief and gratitude.

That evening, Vosikeri arranged for everything to be prepared for Nagasheshu's viva. He called the clerk and confirmed that they would be ready in two days. Meanwhile, Vosikeri reflected on how Beerappa 's birth and the events unfolding were interconnected.

The next day, Nagasheshu packed his belongings, ready to leave for Bengaluru. Vosikeri, along with one of his students, dropped him at the bus stand. Before leaving, Vosikeri gave Nagasheshu advice, reminding him not to take the criticism of others too seriously and to focus on his goals. "Your efforts will not be in vain," Vosikeri said, "and you will be rewarded for your hard work."

As Nagasheshu boarded the bus, Vosikeri thought to himself that Nagasheshu was a man of great passion, driven not by money but by his deep love for his community and culture. Reading through Beerappa 's story had brought tears to Vosikeri's eyes, and he felt honored to be a part of it.

On his journey to Bengaluru, Nagasheshu reflected on many struggles he had faced in his life the people who mocked at him, the obstacles he had overcome, and the long road from stopping his education in eighth grade to achieving his doctorate degree. He felt gratitude towards the helping hands that showed the righteous path.

As planned, Nagasheshu reached in Bengaluru, and completed his viva successfully. Early the next morning, Vosikeri sent him a congratulatory note along with a newspaper clipping that read, "Doctorate for the Shepherd Boy." Vosikeri urged him to come back to Tirupati, where he would be celebrated for his achievement. Nagasheshu, overwhelmed with emotion,gave credited to his parents,  family, and  brothers for being his true motivation. He promised to return to Tirupati in two days for celebration. However, Vosikeri remained anxious, wondering if Nagasheshu would actually return.  True to his word, Nagasheshu traveled to Garimekalapalli, where he shared the joy of his accomplishment with his family. From there, he went to Hindupur the following day, where he received his Ph.D. He also took blessings from Krishnakumari, the woman who had supported him throughout his journey. Later, he was honored with a shawl by the presidents of the *Tapanasahityavedika*, who congratulated him at Sadlapallechidambara Reddy's house.  After celebrating with his family and community, Nagasheshu boarded a bus to Tirupati, arriving early in the morning. Vosikeri welcomed him and took him to his allotted room, where he rested.

The next day, filled with newfound energy and determination, Nagasheshu began writing again, continuing his work on Beerappa 's story, ready to take on the next chapter of his life.

The butchers, upon hearing the terrified screams of the *Sulagithas,* panicked. Their confidence wavered, and doubts began to creep into their minds. The *Sulagithas*, who were sent to execute the dreadful plan, had been captured and tortured, their eyelids burned as punishment. The Rappa people suspected foul play and had begun to gather near the ramparts around the tents, suspecting that something unusual was happening.

The butchers, sensing that something had gone horribly wrong, grew more fearful when they saw the large fire and heard the chaotic noise. They assumed the Rappa people were shooting arrows or readying weapons, and they feared for their lives. "If we stay here, they'll kill us too," they muttered, fleeing from the scene as quickly as they could. They knew Bettappa was dangerous, but now they realized the one who had been born Beerappa  was no ordinary child but destined to be a hero. They thought, "It will be hard to deal with Bettappa if we have failed him."

As they fled through the forest, they encountered a young deer that had fallen to the ground. Desperate to cover their tracks and please Bettappa, they immediately killed the deer, cut off its head, and chopped its body into pieces. They took the meat back to Bettappa, pretending they had fulfilled his gruesome orders.

Bettappa, pleased with their deception, gave them what they had asked for. He cooked the meat with Guttakka, and together they enjoyed their meal, chewing the tender bones down to flour, oblivious to the truth.

Meanwhile, rumors spread quickly throughout the region. News arrived that Meshamandalam thieves had come to Chandragiri to steal sheep but had been killed by the shepherds in the confrontation. Several weeks passed, and one night the Rappa people gathered to celebrate the birth of Barama's son by slaughtering a sheep. The sound of drums and the glow of flames filled the night air, signaling to everyone in the surrounding areas that a great celebration was taking place.

Bettappa, hearing of the celebration, grew curious. He wondered, "What is going on with such a large celebration?" He couldn't help but feel unsettled by the joyous sounds coming from Chandragiri. Despite his attempts to cover up his actions and deceive those around him, Bettappa sensed that something much larger was at play, something he could not control.

To clear that doubt, he called Poddunnekoravanji and asked.

Koravanji heard that he also attended the ceremony that night.

When Koravanji is asked why he throw  such a big party, Koravanji tells the shocking truth.

Ayya said that due to Barama's inability to have a son in Chandragiri, to share the joy with everyone, Barama made a big celebration and slaughtered sheep for everyone.

Did they say that the child died in womb?

Someone said, the child is actually like Lord Brahma. He has a cone shaped mole on his right leg. Alas, that child will become a Maharjataka, a great hero. He confidently said that when he grew up, he will become as powerful as this planet.

Hearing all these words, Bettappa was speechless. Bettappa is worried now.

He immediately called the butchers. He scolded, "What I am saying is, what have you done? Do you want to cheat me by giving me some beef and getting your rewards by kidnapping the child?"

Then he told the truth.

He wants to end the child anyway.

He would give any amount of money to Koravanji and assigns him the task of destroying the village.

"Oof, I can't."

He warned, "If you don't, I will force you."

Koravanji said, "I can't kill him. If I want to, I will tell him that something bad will happen to the child and tell him to leave the child in the forest."

There is Celebrations happeing for the child who was supposed to die due to previous abuse...

It went as far as doing. "If you do that again, I will not be able to bear it. I will kill him with my hands."

Or he promised to give him whatever wealth he wanted if he picked it up somehow.

Koravanji will be in trouble.  As part of that, Koravanji reaches Chandragiri near Barama's house in the afternoon.

Chandragiri is deserted. Here and there the lambs in the barns are screaming. The dogs are barking. No one is seen outside. Soon Koravanji reached Barama's tent. It is quiet in the main tent.

He peeked into the tent. Suramma is fast asleep, sweaty all over from the heat. She is wiping the sweat that is dripping from time to time in her sleep. She laid the child in the blankets and put a rope like string to the blankets and held it in her hand.

The child is sleeping soundly. she was shaking, and he was lying down again, as if he were breaking up in the middle. While sleeping, the string tied to the child's hand was slipping slowly from his hand.

Koravanji looked around. No one saw that Sun was on fire. The child clenched his fist as if to hit someone.

A conch like spot on the thigh is due to the sun.

He is doing something to himself. Koravanji slowly reached Puyala.

Suramma was wiping the sweat from under her throat with her hand from time to time.

Koravanji is slowly untying the threads tied on top. Unbeknownst to the silent period, he lowered the blankets on which the child was lying. He took the mutton from the pot next to him and put it in the sacks he had brought.

He looked around carefully to confirm there is no one around and took small steps. From there, he walked a little way further. He came away from the fire and sat under a tree for shade, hung the boy's clothes on a branch above, and went to the nearby pool, washed his hands, and opened his mouth to eat the meat he had taken from Suramma.

He eats to relive his hunger. He went to the pool again to drink water. Just then, the small child woke up and started crying as if calling for  someone.

Adivanna, who was sleeping on the other side under the same tree, woke up and looked. A child was crying on the tree cradle. He went closer and looked at it. The handsome child was sweet to look at, with the conch like spot on his thigh shining brightly. He looked around suspiciously as to why the child was here, but he did not see anyone. It seemed as if someone had abducted the child and wanted to sell it or kill it. He took the child in the wool and went to the bushes in the forest. When Adivanna picked up the child, the child became silent.

When Koravanji came back, he could not see the baby hanging on the tree cradle. He said, "No!" He looked around and searched all the nearby bushes. Not even a trace was found anywhere. He went to the pool again. He looked around but did not see the child. Bettappa had said that if he brought the child born to Barama, he would give him wealth. Now that his life was in danger, he was pleading with God to show him a way out of this trap.

Adivanna, who was in the nearby bushes, heard this. "Oh!" he thought, "this child is the same one Bettappa is looking to kill." He picked up the child and walked in to  the forest, thinking that if he approached the child's mother again, they would kill her.

Suramma woke up in shock. She got up and looked out. There was no one Immediately, she saw the blankets next to her. There was no baby, but there were strings tied to the blankets. She screamed loudly. The old Mudamma who was in the next hut came running  out to see what had happened.

Suramma screamed there.

Everyone seemed to have missed the moment. No one understood what had happened, but when the baby disappeared from the blankets, everyone understood.

When her husband came in the evening, she didn't know what to say and collapsed, unable to speak. The people around them understood. A few others fearfully searched the surrounding areas to see if the child had been caught by a dog or a fox. The child was nowhere to be found.

Hearing the words of the people who came and said that an animal had entered the tent and taken the child, she cried profusely. She didn't know what to say, and no one understood what had happened. She was suffering in various ways. She was worried about what to say to her husband when he came in the evening.she is Crying profusely. Everyone was consoling her, saying that she was not at fault and that she had no debt to pay.

Meanwhile, the sun seemed to have calmed down a bit. It was reaching towards the west like a cave.

Adivanna walked and walked and reached Kalgiri. There, Lingaya's wife Gauri had a baby, and it was said that someone had left the baby in the forest. He asked her to nurture the baby.

He promised Gauri that the boy would grow up to become a good man.

Gauri and Lingaya accepted the boy as a gift from God. They named him Beerappa . Gauri was already raising another child there, but since that day, Lingaya's wife, Gauri, took care of Beerappa without tending to the sheep anymore.

That evening, Barama, who had not seen his son with his own eyes since the incident, went to the sheep pens and walked past the tent. People had gathered in front of his house. Sensing that something had happened, he hurried inside. Suramma saw her husband and immediately burst into tears.

Barama, trembling, asked the people around what had happened, When he realized his child was missing, he collapsed. Both Barama and Suramma cried loudly, their grief overwhelming them. They screamed in anguish together.

The neighbors filled him in on what had transpired. Barama was distraught, wondering if a snake or a fox had come and taken the child away. He searched frantically, hoping to find at least a trace, a bone or a mark, but there was nothing. His despair deepened, thinking he had married Suramma only to face this heartbreak.

No matter how much they searched, they couldn't find the child. That night, Barama couldn't sleep as he lay near the sheep, his mind filled with thoughts of the child. He felt angry at his wife for leaving the child unprotected. He cursed their fate. The villagers tried to console him, saying there was nothing to be done for the lost child.

Meanwhile, Umadevi, having reached Lingaya's tents with her own child, had no idea where to go or what to do. She prayed to her god Gongadappa, wondering how she could keep going while carrying the baby. Eventually, she collapsed from exhaustion.

She ate whatever food she could find, holding the baby tightly in her arms, fearful of thieves and wild animals lurking around. She had only a small stick to protect herself and feared something worse a thief, a wild animal, or a bull might attack.

She continued walking for days until she spotted a tent in the distance, perched on a hill. With a mix of hope and fear, she headed toward it. Gauri was sitting near the tent, eating some straw. The dogs began barking, sensing someone approaching. Gauri came out and saw a woman carrying something in both hands.

"A woman is in trouble," she thought. She sent the dogs away and called for Lingaya, who shooed them off. Umadevi, driven by her motherly affection, walked slowly but determinedly toward the tent. As soon as she arrived, she collapsed at the entrance.

Gauri rushed out, seeing the woman in distress. She didn't ask any questions but quickly offered her some boiled roots. Umadevi's body was dry from thirst, and the baby cried for milk. Gauri realized the child was hungry, so she hurried to get milk from the sheep.

Lingaya helped her. Gauri took the child from Umadevi and fed him milk. After drinking, the baby fell asleep, content.

Umadevi felt a sense of relief, thinking that she had finally found some support. Somewhere deep within her, there was a flicker of hope for her child's survival. With some food in her stomach, she began to cry, mourning her loss and the immense pain of losing everything right before her eyes. Slowly, she began to share her story with Gauri and Lingaya.

"We used to live near Komalikonda," she started. "My husband Mallanna and Kariappa wife IEswaramma, and we made our living by tending sheep. We had over seven hundred sheep, as well as cows and horses. All the people in the area used to worship the god Gongadappa and make a living through their work.

Many herdsmen from nearby villages would gather to play offerings for Gongadappa. Life was good, and people were happy. But for several years, the rains stopped, and a terrible drought took hold of our region. It became almost impossible to feed the sheep.

Even though we didn't want to leave the place, we had no choice but to move because there was no way to survive. Many families, including ours, left with their sheep.

We climbed to the top of Makutumbam, near Komalikonda. On our way, we found good pasture at the base of Manichula mountain, so we pitched our tents there for a few days and let the sheep graze. For a while, things improved. The sheep were eating well, and we felt some relief after the long drought.

I started thinking that perhaps we should move to a more permanent place, somewhere closer to a community. Mallanna, too, suggested that if we could settle in a place surrounded by neighbors, it would be better. But day after day, we delayed our decision and stayed there.

One night, under the full moon, everyone was sleeping outside. I was in labor, screaming in pain, but no one was around to help. To ward off wild animals, Budabukka was beating a drum to keep them at bay.

Unfortunately, Punikasura and Mallasura, two notorious thieves who roamed the Manichula Mountains, heard the sound. Their sole intention was to steal, and they knew people must be nearby with their sheep. They came down to attack us, knowing that we had valuable livestock. My sister Eswaramma tried to console me as I screamed in pain. In the middle of the night, I gave birth to a baby boy. We named him Malinga, carrying a heavy burden but hoping for a better future.

In the excitement of the baby's birth, everyone let their guard down and relaxed in the tent. The dogs began barking, but no one paid attention. Mallanna and Kariappa were exhausted and slept near the fire. I don't know when I drifted off to sleep, but I did.

At daybreak, Manikasura and Mallasura returned, bringing several men with them while we were still in deep sleep. The dogs started barking again, and the thieves used bamboo sticks to force their way into our camp. The dogs ran in all directions, trying to fend them off. Mallanna and Kariappa woke up in alarm, only to discover that the thieves had broken into the flock of sheep.

They grabbed axes and tried to fight off the thieves, but Manikasura and Mallasura's group was too large. No matter how hard they fought, Mallanna and Kariappa couldn't hold them off. The thieves took all of our sheep and, in the chaos, attacked Mallanna and Kariappa with their long sticks.As the attack continued, Mallanna and Kariappa were overwhelmed, and eventually, they were killed. Eswaramma, who had been crying for help, was also captured. By the time I understood what was happening, it was too late. Everyone was gone or dead.

Fearing for my baby's life, I grabbed him and ran into the bushes. I didn't scream, terrified that the thieves would kill me and my child, too."

After they left, and when the noise of the dogs began to quiet down, I went near the shacks and saw the horror unfolding. They were beating people as if they were venting their anger. I looked around, and everything was barren. Even the thieves who were in the process of killing had taken the sheep and left. It was all falling apart. Two souls had fallen as if they had been torn apart. The men of Manikasura's group were lying wherever they had fallen, cut down by the blows. I cried, holding my husband's lifeless body. The child in my arms also cried, sensing that his father was dead.

As I looked at my child, my heart ached even more. I could see the blood of some of the dogs, stoned by the attackers, flowing on the ground. Stones were scattered in heaps. I don't even know how I managed to leave that place; my body was completely drained of strength. But I found something deep within me, and for the sake of my baby, I survived. Fear haunted me fear of being alone and dying. But my house god, Gongadappa, must have brought me here. When I saw your tents, I felt a flicker of life return. I shared the entire tragedy that had befallen me with you."

Gauri and Lingaya, listening to Umadevi's story, felt deeply saddened by her suffering.

"We are here for you," they told her. "You don't have to go anywhere. You have us."

Lingaya added, "I have enough sheep for you to tend to. Stay here with us today, and take care of the sheep," and left her with the animals. Gauri took great care of Umadevi, and as the weeks passed, Umadevi began to recover. Eventually, Lingaya built her a small tent from the branches and leaves he had gathered in the forest. Umadevi stayed with them, living alongside the others in the area.

Meanwhile, Manikasura and Mallasura, accompanied by Eswaramma, continued to roam the land, grazing their stolen sheep and killing them whenever they pleased. The sheep moved up the hills and down the valleys, but Eswaramma's condition had become worse than the sheep's. Whenever the band of thieves felt like it, they would attack and plunder. At first, only Manikasura and Mallasura led these attacks, but soon their followers joined in, making their raids more frequent and more brutal.

The thieves continued to graze the sheep in different places for a few days at a time. During this time, a disease called Segadommaroga struck the cows, causing them to collapse where they stood. Even the sheep began to fall in piles, and Manikasura was at a loss. He thought long and hard about what to do, but no matter what he did, the sheep kept dying some from blood loss.

Frustrated, Manikasura turned to Eswaramma and asked, "What's happening? Why are the sheep dying like this?"

Eswaramma, filled with sorrow, replied, "It's not just the sheep that are suffering. You and your men have stolen everything. You've killed the people and left us without families. My younger sister, Ninduchulalu, passed away just the other day, and I don't even know where my mother is now whether she's alive or not. She could be wandering somewhere with my little niece, or they may have been left as food for wild animals. Our clan will surely be punished for all the evil you've done. Somewhere, a brave man will rise, and he will seize your sheep and crush your games. If you go near him, you will die at his hands, and his dogs will tear you apart."

Mallasura, confident and dismissive, rejected Eswaramma's warning. "No one has the courage to face us," he said, convinced of their invincibility.

Soon after, Manikasura's group arrived near Mashanadu with their flock of sheep.

At the same time, Bettappa had been wandering through the area, looking at every tree, searching for a place to worship his cattle. As he searched, he heard the sound of bubbling drums. When Bettappa drew closer to the sound, he came face to face with Manikasura. Bettappa was shocked and terrified to see him.

Manikasura, noticing Bettappa wandering around the trees early in the day, asked him, "Why are you wandering around so early?"

Bettappa replied, "I have been worshiping Pasupatalaya every day. God is highly revered, and therefore I've made it a part of my daily routine to worship Him."

Manikasura, curious, asked, "Where is this Almighty God?"

Bettappa pointed and said, "If you look from here, you will see Him on that hill."

Manikasura then asked, "Why are the sheep just standing there? Is there someone here who knows what's best for them?"

Bettappa responded, "You must not forget your household god. First, pray to your household god, and if you ask, he will tell you the solution."

Manikasura asked, "Where does this god live?"

Bettappa replied, "He wanders here and there, without any fixed place. Wherever he is, he confronts whatever comes his way, stronger than anyone else. You can face him too."

Manikasura then said, "If you're worshiping the temple every day, then why don't you know what to do?"

Bettappa, sensing something, asked, "Where do you come from?"

Manikasura replied, "We are coming from Manyakhetam."

Hearing the name Manyakhetam, Bettappa was shocked. He tried to distance himself from Manikasura, thinking he might be seeking compensation for something.

Manikasura noticed this and asked, "Are you trying to get away from me out of fear?"

Bettappa, now cautious, responded, "We will do whatever is necessary, just tell us what you need."

Bettappa said, "In our house, we treat Adivanna like god. They are always attentive to us. Once, when my sheep were stricken with a disease, I asked our household god for help and offered him a small sacrifice. As soon as I did that, the disease disappeared from my flock. It was diminished. Well, tell me, no matter what, we will get rid of anyone who stands in our way."

The first name that came to Bettappa's mind was "Beerappa ." Manikasura continued, "It is said that if you sacrifice a man with a conch shaped mark on his thigh, your flock will be saved from being slaughtered."

Bettappa asked, "What is he doing now?"

Manikasura responded, "I don't know where he is, but if we find him and kill him, no one else will be able to stand against us."

Bettappa, deep in thought, replied, "You mentioned that God Pashupati is highly revered, and yet you who worship Him are not enough."

Manikasura then demanded, "Tell me, who is the priest who conducts the worship for this god? I will bless him myself."

Bettappa, thinking carefully, said inwardly, "Someone will eventually try to kill me." Aloud, he said, "Ayya, I am not the priest who enters the sanctum and worships."

Manikasura asked, "Then tell me, who is the priest?"

Bettappa mentioned Barama, his sister's husband, and told him, "He is the one you seek."

Manikasura asked, "And where does he live?"

Bettappa replied, "If you walk towards Chandragiri, anyone you ask will tell you where Barama lives."

Manikasura then insisted, "No, you should come with us as well."

Bettappa, trying to stall, said, "I am going to gather clover flowers." But Manikasura, raising his axe threateningly, said, "If you don't come with us, I'll kill you before you can gather those flowers."

Reluctantly, Bettappa followed them, saying, "Ayya, I will surely come."

With that, everyone, including the herd of sheep, began walking away, with the sheep trailing along the path.

Manikasura and Mallasura explained that their cattle had been stolen and everyone who tried to resist had been cut down. They proudly proclaimed themselves as notorious thieves, feared by all.

Bettappa, witnessing all of this, grew increasingly anxious. However, he knew that the one they intended to kill was no ordinary man. He warned them, "He's too strong for you to kill directly. You'll need to find another way. Remember, this is the same man who killed

Konasura and Mundasura earlier. You need a different approach to take him down." Bettappa advised them carefully.

Manikasura raised his ax again, as if demanding more answers. "You must know something about what you're advising," he pressed.

Bettappa, sensing the danger, quickly suggested, "Ayya, you should seek blessings from your household god. Don't you all know how deeply devoted shepherds are to their gods? Call upon them to seek divine blessings, and this will give you a way to proceed."

As expected, both Manikasura and Mallasura arrived at Chandragiri and introduced themselves to Barama. They explained, "We have come here to graze our sheep, but our herd is being plagued by some mysterious sickness, and many are dying. We need to offer a sacrifice to the household god. Everyone knows that godliness is life, so we have come to ask you to join us in worship and participate in this ritual."

Barama asked, "Have you informed the surrounding shepherds?"

Manikasura replied, "Yes, we have told all the shepherds nearby."

Satisfied with their response, Barama agreed to take part in the ritual.

Meanwhile, Umadevi, sitting quietly with her sheep, would occasionally clap her hands, tousle her hair, and laugh loudly to herself. She would mutter that she had nothing but her sheep for her livelihood. Her strange behavior frightened the people around her. They believed she was possessed, thinking the devil had come upon her, and worried that her unpredictable actions could bring misfortune to the village.

Fearing her outbursts, the villagers asked what she wanted. Umadevi declared, "If I don't sacrifice animals, I will not find peace."

As a result, many animals were sacrificed. The meat from these sacrifices was dried and eaten as a means of survival.

Time passed, and Umadevi continued raising her son Malinga, who had now reached the age where he could play with other children. Nagappa, Lingaiah, and Mayamma children who had grown up in the village often played with Malinga. Malinga and

Mayamma, especially, became close playmates, even though Mayamma was slightly older than Malinga.

Bettappa's daughter, too, had grown old enough to play with the other children. She was being cared for with great love and attention. Even Beerappa,now old enough to play, became a part of their little circle of children. Bettappa was happy to see his daughter and Beerappa thriving, though there remained a lingering fear deep inside him especially after what had happened when Koravanji tried to take Beerappa . But now, Bettappa knew that the entire village had heard Suramma's painful cries about being childless, and this knowledge allowed him to remain calm.

Despite his outward calmness, Bettappa had secretly planned to kill his brother in law, Barama. He believed that with the help of Manikasura and Mallasura, they would be able to kill him, no matter the circumstances. Bettappa was confident that the thieves would carry out his plan.

Preparations for the ritual to honor Gongadappa were made in secret. Bettappa, the mastermind behind the entire plot, kept everything hidden. He carefully ensured that no one suspected his involvement with Manikasura and Mallasura. He reveled in his success and felt satisfied, knowing that Suramma was the last remaining obstacle. He believed that Koravanji would eventually find a way to kill Beerappa .

Together, Manikasura, Mallasura, and Eswaramma prepared the sacrificial ritual. A three faccd yellow stone was placed at the center of the ritual site, adorned with garlands made of Chuttoora leaves. The entire area was decorated with sheep's wool, beautifully arranged to signify the solemnity of the occasion.

Finally, Barama arrived at the shearing place, where the ritual was to take place. He came to offer his prayers and perform the sacrificial worship. Unbeknownst to him, the wheels of a sinister plot had already been set in motion.

All the pujas are done according to the custom. Barama is standing and watching everything

He asked if none of Rappa's men had come yet.

Manikasura said that they will come but no one has come yet.

He called forward that you will bring prasadam.Barama moved a little forward from where he was standing, Mallasura gave prasadam. Behind Barama is Manikasura. Barama takes the prasad with both hands and looks at his eyes from his head. Manikasura, who was behind, cut Barama from behind with his ax. That's when Barama collapsed. He fell holding the Prasad with both hands. He closed his eyes as if a large banyan tree had been uprooted by the wind and fell down, shouting "Mama". The flamboyant Bettappa squealed with uncontrollable joy. The Manikasuras pushed all the sheep of Barama and left from there.

Beerappa is improving day by day. Always Playing, and jumping , he is more talented than all the children in the house. Catching Beerappa became a headache for Lingaiah, Gauri and Mayamma.

Mother, this child is like a son to you, it is your responsibility to take care of this boy, it is enough that we are shepherding the sheep. He said, "So we are taking care of him." He told his mother that you should take care of this child so that you two should meet forever.

Also, my grandmother is taking care of all the wellbeing of her brother.

Mayamma is older than Beerappa and Malinga comes to play with Beerappa . All three are playing together.

When Mayamma and Beerappa grew a bit older, Lingaya's flock of sheep increased, so Gauri and Lingaya along with Maaymma were taken to the sheepfold.

Beerappa is going after them saying that I too will come to the sheep.

They say you will be playing here. Beerappa said that if I am there, I will come too, and he goes after the sheep.

One day when a sheep was being milked, Lingayya would chase the herd from Beerappa near the sheep. Just at that time, the wolf came and the wolf went without grabbing the lamb that was still suckling. Beerappa caught the legs of the lamb. The wolf is pulling forward and Beerappa is pulling back. The wolf has been snatched away. Beerappa, who has caught the sheep, keeps fllowing behind trying to hold its hind legs.

The wolf is screaming loudly. Beerappa also kept shouting loudly but the sheep did not leave. Meanwhile, the dogs and Lingaya came running and freed the sheep. Lingaya was very touched to see the baby holding its hindlegs and not letting go no matter what. How dare you, Lingayyya was afraid of what would happen if the wolf was a sheep and caught you. He wanted to become a big hero.

Guttakka named the child Kannikamala Devi. According to custom, the boy was named Palappa in Meshanadu and left Tagaru.

The tiger walked and stood two times further than the front of the bush.

Everyone was surprised by the events unfolding. Everything had been done according to tradition, but many began to believe that something was wrong with Beerappa . Some wondered aloud if the child was cursed or if it was the village's fate to bear the burden of this unusual situation. Others suggested that Beerappa should be offered as a servant (dasi) to the village to balance the scales.

The elders of the village speaks that  , "There must be a reason for all this, or else we should leave everything to God's will. Whatever is happening, there is a purpose behind it." Kannikamamaladevi, who had never married again, was particularly distressed.

Gudenjanam spread rumors throughout the village, claiming that there was something fundamentally wrong with the child. Guttakka, sensing danger for Beerappa,began raising the child in isolation, hidden from everyone. Beerappa was kept indoors, away from the other children, and forbidden from interacting with anyone. There were no toys, no playmates nothing but the tents he lived in.

As Beerappa grew older, he became increasingly restless. One day, he saw the other children playing with a game called Chillakatti and insisted that he wanted to play too. Guttakka reluctantly allowed him to join. However, during the game, Beerappa hit another child on the head, causing him to bleed. The child ran back to the tent to tell his parents, and soon, a commotion erupted in the village. All the surrounding villagers blamed Lingaya for Beerappa 's behavior.

Amid the chaos, the situation suddenly calmed down when Lingaya declared, "This child is a gift from God, and I cannot punish him." Beerappa continued to live as he wished, refusing to listen to anyone. His reckless behavior escalated, causing problems for everyone.

Every day, Beerappa s games brought more trouble. His mother, Gauri, was often end up cleaning homes after he finishes his games and forgoing his mistakes. Beerappa would run to the water holes and play pranks, throwing mud into the buckets of those fetching water. Sometimes it was broken glass; other times, it was a blow to someone's head. The villagers struggled to handle his mischief, and each day brought new complaints.

Rumors began to spread even more fiercely: "A child without parents, raised with no discipline, will bring ruin. He doesn't even know what he's doing." Despite these rumors, Lingaiah and Gauri continued to care for Beerappa as best they could, marveling at his growth.

One day, a group of women from the village came to Lingaiah's house, intending to punish him for Beerappa s actions. Lingaiah, in his calm manner, told them, "Yes, the child has made the mistakes, and I will make sure to correct him." His words calmed them down, and they left.

After the villagers left, Lingaiah scolded Beerappa for his reckless behavior. Beerappa, sensing the seriousness, refrained from playing his usual games for a few years, instead choosing to spend his time near the Rappaladagga or Gorelo, where the shepherds gathered.

One day, the children were playing with arrows inside the house, and Beerappa saw them. He argued with his grandmother, saying, "I want an arrow too!" His grandmother, fearing what trouble might come from it, hesitated. "It's not that I don't want to give you an arrow," she said, "but we need to wait for your father. He will decide."

When evening came, Beerappa rushed to Lingaiah, insisting, "I want a real arrow, like the ones hunters use. I want to hunt." Lingaiah replied, "Okay, I will make one for you. We need a bamboo stick. Tomorrow, when we go out to the sheep hearding, I'll get the bamboo and make the iron rod for the arrow."

Beerappa was appeased for the moment, and he slept peacefully that night.

The next morning, before anyone was awake, Malinga and Beerappa sneaked out into the forest without telling anyone. Umadevi, Malinga's mother, came looking for him at Lingaya's house, but neither of the boys could be found. Panic spread through the village. The villagers searched everywhere, but the boys were nowhere to be seen.

Eventually, someone spotted them near a cave, one that was known to be dangerous because it often caught fire. Fear gripped the villagers, thinking that a fight might break out or that something terrible could happen. But to everyone's astonishment, Malinga and Beerappa were playing with tiger cubs inside the cave.

The two boys emerged from the cave, carrying the cubs in their arms. The entire village stood there, watching in awe and disbelief.

After playing with the tiger cubs and being scolded for it, Beerappa and Malinga left the cubs behind and ran back home, terrified. Once home, they cried, "We don't want the puppies!" But everyone knew these were not just puppies they were tiger cubs. The adults were horrified, knowing that if the tiger had seen them with its cubs, it could have torn the children apart.

Lingaiah and Gauri were in shock, discussing how narrowly the boys had escaped danger. "It's frightening to think what could have happened if they had gone deeper into the cave," they said.

One day, while Adivanna was clearing his throat, he came across Lingaiah. Adivanna inquired about the children, and Lingaiah explained the trouble Beerappa had been causing. Adivanna warned him, "Your nephew is looking for Beerappa,and he plans to kill him. You need to be careful."

Lingaiah also shared his concerns about Beerappa 's mischief, saying, "I don't know how to guide him. He refuses to listen."

Adivanna, offering advice, said, "There is a way to change his behavior. If you bring cassava flowers and crushed nuts to the Nagara well and worship the new moon at the Pashupati temple, the child will change significantly."

Lingaiah asked, "Where is this Nagara well?"

Adivanna replied, "It's deep in a valley under the distant hills. It's a very deep well, and you must go there to collect the flowers."

Determined to help his son, Lingaiah set out to find the Nagara well, taking Beerappa,Gauri, and Mayamma along to care for the sheep on the way. After searching for a long time, they finally spotted the deep well. The sight of it terrified Lingaiah. It was incredibly deep, with twisted vines and roots hanging into it. The water below seemed dark as glass, and it looked as though it belonged in the underworld.

The flowers Adivanna had mentioned were there, but no signs of any human presence could be seen. Lingaiah was struck with fear. "If I go down, will I be able to come back up?" he wondered. He felt uncertain, and no one was nearby to help. He realized that if something went wrong, he would be alone and unable to call for aid. With a heavy heart, Lingaiah returned home, leaving the task to God. That night, Lingaiah told Gauri everything that had happened. However, to his surprise, by evening, Beerappa had somehow brought the flowers Lingaiah had been too scared to collect. No one knew how he had managed to do it. Despite the worship and offerings made with the flowers, there was no change in Beerappa 's behavior. Days turned into months, months into years, yet Beerappa remained as playful and reckless as ever. His energy never waned, and his thirst for adventure only grew stronger. Eventually, Beerappa insisted, "I want to learn archery."

In her eagerness to help, Maamma made a small bow and arrow for him. In the village of Gudem, Siddaiah, an expert in archery, was teaching children how to use bows. Beerappa,along with Maamma and Malinga, went to learn archery from Siddaiah.

Siddaiah showed the children how to aim properly, explaining the techniques of shooting arrows. When it was Beerappa 's turn, he picked up the bow, aimed, and hit the target perfectly on his first try. Siddaiah was astonished. "This boy has the talent of a hero," he thought. "Perhaps he is destined for greatness."

Within less than a week, Beerappa,filled with excitement, called Malinga and went off hunting in the nearby forest. One day, they ventured into the hills near Meshanadu, where tigers roamed. Hunting in these hills required immense courage, as the animals there, like the mechani, were fierce and had serrated spines.

But Beerappa, without hesitation, shot his arrow and struck one of the mechani. The creature screeched and darted into the bushes, and Beerappa, undeterred, followed it into the forest.

Beerappa, filled with a fierce energy, grabs the creature (the dangerous "Mechani") that was retreating into the bushes and stomps it down with his feet. As this happens, Bettappa witnesses Beerappa 's astonishing strength, seeing him defeat the mechani and then kill a tiger nearby. Bettappa, in disbelief, realizes that there are no hunters capable of such feats around here. He begins to inquire about the child's identity.

The shepherds around tell him, "That's Lingaya's son, Beerappa." This information confuses Bettappa because he knows Lingaya has been childless. A deep suspicion starts growing in his mind: could this boy be his sister's son?

The villagers speak in awe of Godopa, the deadly hunter of Mekas. "Its claws are more terrifying than a tiger's, its wings sharper than any needle, and its bite can kill any man or animal," they say. Yet Beerappa remains unafraid, staying close to Rappa and avoiding hunting for now.

Every day, the children who are learning archery compete to see how far they can shoot their arrows. Beerappa, not yet allowed to join in, watches from the side. As he watches, a thought forms in his mind:  they think they're shooting far, but none of them can compete with me.

Finally, Beerappa decides to enter the competition. "Who will compete with me?" he asks boldly. The other children, unsure, respond. Some refuse, but others are curious and eager to see Beerappa shoot.

The children begin taking turns, shooting their arrows high into the air and watching how far they travel. When Beerappa 's turn comes, he shoots his arrow with all his might, and it soars into the sky, much higher than anyone else's. All the children watch in amazement, their eyes wide open. The arrow climbs higher and higher, seemingly never coming down.

As they continue to look up, suddenly the arrow starts descending, like a bird diving toward its prey. But something goes horribly wrong the arrow strikes a boy in the eye, plunging deep into it. The boy lets out a piercing scream, thrashing on the ground, his arms and legs flailing. The other children, horrified by the sight, run in fear to tell the adults what had happened. Some rush to the sheep pens, while others sprint to Beerappa 's house to alert Mayamma.

Mayamma, hearing the news, rushes to the scene. She finds the boy on the ground, bleeding profusely from his eye. Without hesitation, she pulls the arrow from his eye, but blood continues to flow. Desperate, she throws dirt into the wound and presses leaves against it, trying to stop the bleeding. But nothing seems to work the blood keeps gushing.

The boy's screams echo through the village, drawing a crowd. The entire village soon knows about the incident, and the news spreads quickly. In the evening, when the sheep return to their pens, all the children tell their families what happened.

The boy's father, devastated, runs to his injured son, crying out, "Oh, what an injustice!" He gathers some villagers and rushes to Lingaya's tent, bringing firewood with them, ready to confront him.

When Lingaiah learns what has happened, he realizes the danger Beerappa is in. He quickly tells Beerappa to hide somewhere far away, knowing the villagers are seeking revenge. Those who come to Lingaiah's tent break down the barriers, pushing their way in and attacking him. They search everywhere for Beerappa, but he is nowhere to be found. Frustrated and furious, they vow to kill Beerappa when they find him.

Inside, Lingaiah lies wounded, and Gauri weeps, wondering what to do with Beerappa . She fears that ever since Beerappa came into their lives, trouble has followed. They wonder if it would be better for Beerappa to leave the village for good, to avoid further conflict.

That night, neither Mayamma nor Malinga could sleep. Anxiety hung heavy in the air, and no one knew where Beerappa had gone to hide in the forest.

Beerappa, somewhere deep in the forest,  remained hidden, his whereabouts unknown to anyone.

Beerappa remained invisible, hiding from the village and everyone who sought him. Meanwhile, the child who had been struck by the arrow continued to worsen. Day by day, the child's vision deteriorated. They tried various remedies, applying some kind of mortar to the wound, but the swelling wouldn't go down, and the child was slowly going blind.

Bettappa, hearing about the boy who had hunted the tiger and the dangerous mechani, made his way to Kalgiri, intent on finding him. When Bettappa arrived, Lingaiah was preparing a fire. Sensing something, Bettappa questioned Lingaiah: "Don't you have sons or daughters? You have two other children, don't you? Where are they?"

Lingaiah, caught off guard, stuttered and hesitated. "What are you asking?" he said nervously.

Bettappa pressed, and Lingaiah finally admitted, "Both of them are my children."

Bettappa wasn't satisfied and demanded the truth. Under pressure, Lingaiah explained that Adivanna had brought them, one boy and one girl, both found abandoned in the forest.

Maayamma overheard this conversation. She was shocked to learn the truth that she and Beerappa were not Lingaya's biological children. Even Lingaiah didn't realize Maamma had heard this revelation.

Maayamma immediately set out to find Adivanna, determined to learn the truth. However, no one knew where Adivanna was or when he would reappear.

Despite the uncertainty, Maayamma now knew that she and Beerappa were not truly Lingaiah's children.

Bettappa, driven by his suspicions, also left Kalgiri in search of Adivanna. On his journey, Bettappa encountered Adivanna along the way. They exchanged words, and Adivanna revealed the truth to Bettappa: Beerappa and Maamma were not Lingaiah's children, but Beerappa was the son of Bettappa's younger sister.

"You have come to claim what is yours," Adivanna told Bettappa, "and Beerappa is your sister's son." He even challenged Bettappa to take care of his sister's son properly and demanded that Bettappa arrange Maamma's marriage.

Bettappa, enraged, returned to Kalgiri, determined to act. Confronting Lingaiah, he shouted, "The child growing up near you is none other than the son of my younger sister! You have no right to him! You also killed their father!"

Lingaiah, shocked by the accusation, pleaded his innocence. "Oh, why would I do that? I don't know anything about this!" he cried.

Bettappa, however, threatened him, saying, "If I don't find Beerappa,I will tell everyone the truth. I will tell the village that you committed that crime!"

Lingaiah, desperate, promised, "Aiya, Beerappa is my responsibility. I will search for him wherever he is. Please, don't doubt me."

Even Gauri, his wife, stood in disbelief and fear.

They searched for Beerappa far and wide, but no one could find him. After weeks of searching, Bettappa, furious, returned and threatened Lingaiah again: "If you see him, bring him to me! If not, I will kill you."

Beerappa, wherever he had been wandering, stayed away for several months, hidden from everyone. He knew danger awaited him if he returned.

Later, when Beerappa finally came back to Kalgiri to see his grandmother, the villagers, still angry over the incident with the blind child, gathered together. Word spread quickly, and they wanted to exact revenge on Beerappa . They brought firewood, intending to beat him when they found him.

Despite Lingaiah and Gauri's desperate attempts to stop them, even begging on their knees, the villagers refused to listen. Both Lingaiah and Gauri were injured in their efforts to protect Beerappa, and Lingaiah, furious, rejected the villagers' demands.

The villagers, now hostile, set a rule: "You must leave! Either you send them away, or we will force you to vacate this place."

Gauri, who had raised Beerappa and Mayamma with the love of a mother, though she hadn't birthed them, was heartbroken. Both children were devastated, their hearts torn apart by the events.

Their eyes seemed to speak, as though they were telling each other, *It's not because of us, but we must leave. We can't stay here anymore.

Both Mayamma and Beerappa had silently decided not to trouble their father, Lingaiah. That night, they left the house without a word, vacating it quietly. Lingaiah, as usual, tried to search for Beerappa the next morning, but both children were gone. When dawn broke, Lingaiah realized they had vanished. Overcome with grief, he burst into tears, having always considered the two children as blessings in his life. Now, with both of them missing, his heart ached in a way he couldn't bear.

Gauri, trying to comfort him, said, "There is no debt to repay. It's not your fault." But as a mother, her own heart was shaken.

Meanwhile, Mayamma and Beerappa walked deeper into the forest, surviving on various fruits and wild edibles they found along the way cotton nuts, kalivi nuts, gadiri nuts, palm fruits, guavas, jackfruits, wild bananas, and many others. Their tired bodies eventually found rest near a small temple by a cave named Kaivanka.

Next to the temple was a well. Beerappa, always restless, decided to swim in it. He stirred the water until it muddied like an elephant's pool, splashing around and scattering flowers from the surrounding trees. While Beerappa busied himself with his antics, Mayamma, exhausted, fell fast asleep under the shade of a nearby tree.

At that moment, the priest who had come to the temple to perform puja spotted Mayamma. Seeing the young girl asleep, he hatched a sinister plan. He thought he could abduct her and sell her to the wealthy Lord Bhagwanthappa in Mungisur. Without a second thought, he abandoned the items he had brought for the puja and stealthily approached Mayamma.

He carefully picked up Mayamma, who remained asleep. She didn't wake up as he carried her a long distance in silence. When he found a shaded spot, he stopped to rest, and only then did Mayamma begin to stir. When she opened her eyes, she immediately realized she was in danger and tried to scream for help. But the priest quickly covered her mouth, threatening to kill her if she made a sound.

Terrified, Mayamma struggled to break free, but the priest held her tightly, refusing to let go. She felt hopeless, unsure of what was going to happen to her, and all she could think of was escape.

Meanwhile, Bhagwanthappa was being praised by the villagers for his bravery, having supposedly killed a tiger. He had offered the groom of his choice the privilege of choosing any sheep from his flock as a reward.

Back at the well, Beerappa had finished playing in the water. He was tired, hungry, and feeling the fatigue from his mischievous antics. When he looked around for his sister under the tree where he had left her, she was nowhere to be found. His wet body had dried under the heat of the sun, but his tongue felt parched, and his temper flared as he wondered where Mayamma had gone.

Confused and angry, Beerappa thought, *Where could she have gone?* He reasoned that perhaps she had wandered off, but it seemed unlikely. He shouted her name loudly, thinking she might hear him. But there was no answer, and now Beerappa grew even more anxious.

As the gravity of the situation began to sink in, Beerappa thought to himself, *What if something happened to her while I was swimming?* A deep suspicion gnawed at him, making him wonder if a wild animal might have taken her. Filled with worry, he immediately started searching the surrounding hills and trees, scanning every possible place where she might be.

Determined, Beerappa set off to find his sister, suspecting something terrible had happened in the forest.

Beerappa realized something was wrong when he saw the items for the puja scattered on the ground. Someone had clearly taken them. He noticed small footprints in the sand and began following them. As he continued, he spotted tents in Mungisuru, far away from Kaivanka, atop a mound. A thought crossed his mind *Maybe my sister is there.* Determined, he made his way toward the small tents.

Inside one of those tents, Mayamma was held captive. Veeru, the grandson of Ray, taunted her, saying, "Your brother Beerappa will come, but even if he does, he can't do anything. I'll beat him and take you back."

Bhagwanthappa, the lord of Mungisuru, calmly responded, "Coming here is not an easy task. It takes more than just bravery."

Mayamma, with confidence, replied, "Beerappa has grown up in adversity, flourishing even near the terrible depths of Nagarabavi. When we were children, he ventured to perform puja at that deep well but was unable to descend. Yet he returned determined, full of strength and courage. He's the one who fought tigers as a child, and he'll come for me."

Bhagwanthappa, unmoved, said, "We'll see about that."

Just as they spoke, Beerappa reached the tents, but the guards refused to let him enter. He saw his sister tied up and in distress. His anger flared, but he kept his calm. He didn't realize that the man holding his sister was Bhagwanthappa, the one they had been talking about. Eventually, after hearing Bhagwanthappa's name, Beerappa calmed down, though the fire in his eyes remained.

Seeing his sister tied to the post, helpless and suffering, Beerappa 's heart broke. He couldn't bear to see her like this. With a voice full of emotion, he pleaded, "Please, let my sister go. Since childhood, she's cared for me like a mother. She's protected me, fed me, and taken care of me. I owe her my life, and I can't imagine her in such a condition. I beg you, let her go. I'll do whatever you want in return."

Bhagwanthappa, smirking, said, "You talk about being a hero, but we want to see your bravery. Show us what you're capable of."

Beerappa, ever composed, responded, "A true hero doesn't hurt others to prove his strength. True bravery is shown when you face danger for a noble cause."

Bhagwanthappa challenged him further, saying, "Show your heroism through preservation. Do something truly heroic, and I'll let your sister go."

Beerappa was confused and asked, "What do you mean by that?"

Bhagwanthappa explained, "My daughter has been suffering from terrible back pain for many years. Everyone here knows it. Many healers have tried various remedies, but nothing has worked. It is said that the only cure is the juice of the *kukkavainti* and *kalasakura* roots soaked in the water of Donakonda Nerri. But no one dares to go there because of the dangers. There's a legend that a ghost of an old woman, Wokamusalamma, haunts the path, warning travelers not to climb the hill, or else they won't return. Even worse, a weeping serpent guards the roots you seek. Many who have gone have never come back."

Beerappa listened carefully, realizing the challenge before him.

Bhagwanthappa continued, "I've heard stories of your childhood, how you faced challenges bravely. Your sister told me you're a hero, so now, prove it. If you want your sister's freedom, you must bring back the water soaked *kukkavainti* and *kalasakura* roots from Donakonda Nerri. Do that, and I'll release your sister. Not only that, but I'll also give you a hundred sheep and a horse as a reward."

Beerappa, knowing that this was the only way to save his sister, stood tall and accepted the challenge. "I will bring what you ask for. My sister's life is more precious than anything," he said.

The stage was now set for Beerappa 's next test of bravery. He knew the journey ahead would be dangerous, but he was ready to face any challenge for Mayamma.

Bhagwanthappa assured Beerappa,"I will take care of your sister without any trouble until you return." He untied the ropes binding Mayamma and set her free.

Mayamma, however, was deeply concerned. She urged Beerappa not to go on such a dangerous journey, saying, "Don't think about me. We can fight them together and escape, or you should leave me here. I don't want you to risk your life on this journey. It's better for me to die than for you to take such a risk."

Beerappa, resolute, responded, "My sister is not different from me; a sister is equal to a mother. How could I leave you behind? Was I born as your younger brother just to abandon you? No, I will either live or die, but I will not leave you."

Mayamma, still worried, said, "Brother, if anything happens to you on this journey, I will never forgive myself. Please, go back."

Beerappa, determined, replied, "I cannot leave you behind as a witness to the Panchabhutalas (the five elements) that are part of this creation. If you are safe, then everything will be fine. I owe it to you, and I will fulfill this responsibility."

Hearing these words, Mayamma's heart sank. She pleaded, "Please, brother, don't talk like that. I will never leave you."

Beerappa then turned to Bhagwanthappa and said, "Aiya, I will bring what you have asked for. But before I go, please give me the horse now." Bhagwanthappa, sensing Beerappa 's determination, handed over the horse to him.

Mayamma, watching her younger brother prepare to leave, was overwhelmed with emotion. She couldn't bear the thought of him going on this perilous journey, fearing that she might never see him again. With tears in her eyes, she confessed, "Beerappa,I must tell you something. You are not really my brother."

Beerappa was stunned. "What? What are you saying, Akka?" he asked, his face full of confusion.

Mayamma, her voice heavy with emotion, explained, "What I am saying is true. You are not my biological brother, and I am not your sister. We were both raised by Lingaya, but we are not his children."

Beerappa, even more shocked, stammered, "But... how can this be?"

Mayamma continued, "Your real parents are Barama and Suramma. You are their child, and your true home is Chandragiri. You belong to a lineage of heroes, Beerappa ."

Beerappa stood in disbelief, his whole world turned upside down.

Mayamma added, "Your great uncle, Bettappa, lives in Meshanadu. He tried to kill you even before you were born, fearing that your birth would bring about his downfall. He attempted many times to take your life. When you were born, he even sent men with steel nails to kill you in your cradle. But no one could stop your arrival on this earth.

Later, he plotted again, planning to kill you with a crowbar. But it was Adivanna who saved you from that trap and brought you to Lingaya. I heard all of this from Lingaya, and your uncle Bettappa, who revealed it. I, too, am not Lingaya's child; I was brought here just like you."

Beerappa was overwhelmed. Tears welled up in his eyes, and for a moment, he couldn't stop crying. His entire life, everything he had believed, was unraveling before him.

Mayamma went on, "Your father was killed by Bettappa, too. When I heard that, I could feel the rage building within you. You belong to a lineage of warriors, Beerappa,and your blood runs hot with the courage of your ancestors."

Beerappas fists clenched in anger, his veins throbbing like the currents of a raging river. The thought of his mother, now lost and directionless in Chandragiri, filled him with a burning determination. His clenched fists felt like they could cut through steel.

But Beerappa calmed himself, resolving to focus on his immediate goal freeing his sister from Bhagwanthappa's clutches.

He looked at Mayamma, his face now resolute, and said, "Before I deal with anything else, I will free you, Akka. No one will keep you captive, not while I am alive."

Beerappa, filled with a deep sense of responsibility and compassion, said to Mayamma, "No matter what the truth is about our birth, you are still my sister in every way that matters. I know how much you've suffered for me, and that bond between us can't be undone. In hard times, it's important to stay close to those we care about, and I am here for you, just as you were always there for me. We don't need pity to share burdens if we have the strength to help, we must do so. And I am your brother, through and through."

He reassured Lord Bhagwanthappa, "I will bring the water soaked *kukkavainta* and *Kalasakuruware* for your daughter."

After hearing  Beerappas story, Bhagwanthappa was moved. His heart softened, and he regretted the harsh treatment of Beerappa,a motherless child who had already suffered so much.

"Aya," Bhagwanthappa said, "after hearing about your birth and how your uncle tried to kill you, I felt like my heart  were being torn apart. I cannot continue to torment a child like you. Take your sister and go. I will honor all the promises I made. You need not prove anything to me."

But Beerappa stood firm. "No, Ayya. I gave my word that I would bring what you asked for, and only then will I return with my sister." He took his sister's blessings and prepared to leave, despite Mayamma's desperate pleas for him not to go. She clung to him, crying, but Beerappa gently freed himself from her embrace and set off on his journey.

Donakonda, the hill he had to climb, was known for being treacherous. Many who had attempted to scale it were scared off by the stories of shepherds who warned of dangers along the way. The mountain loomed tall and ominous in the distance, visible even from Mungisur, like a massive bull standing guard.

Beerappa rode his horse, determined to complete his mission, and arrived at the base of Donakonda as darkness began to fall. As he approached the hill, he encountered an old woman, tending to cows. She was mooing to the animals, but something about her seemed out of place. Beerappa wondered if this was the ghostly figure that Bhagwanthappa had warned him about. But as he got closer, he saw that she was just a frail old woman, shaking as she grazed her cows.

Beerappa greeted her respectfully, "Namaste, Avva."

The old woman looked at him curiously and asked, "Who are you, Nayana? Why are you here?"

Beerappa replied, "I am here on an important mission. Bhagwanthappa's daughter is unwell, and I have come to gather the *kukkavainta* and *Kalasakuruware* roots, soaked in the blue water of Nerri from this hill, to help heal her."

The old woman sighed deeply. "Ah, many have said the same thing before you. But, young man, it would be wise to turn back. Many have tried to climb this hill, and many have lost their lives. No one comes back from that mountain. If you fall into that abyss, you will not be born again."

Beerappa, resolute in his quest, remained unmoved. "Avva, I appreciate your concern, but I cannot turn back. If I leave now, I will return only with those roots."

The old woman sighed again, shaking her head. "Many have ignored my warnings, and none have returned. But you... you seem different. If you truly wish to go, then go with the strength of your resolve. May you succeed where others have failed."

She blessed him, saying, "Shabash, Aiya. You are a true hero. May your bravery bring you glory that will be remembered for ages. You will face great challenges, but I see in you the strength to overcome them. May you live long and prosper."

Beerappa,focused on his mission, thanked the old woman and continued his journey up the mountain, her words of warning and blessing still ringing in his ears. He felt the weight of the task ahead but paid no attention to the dangers she had spoken of. His only thought was to retrieve the roots and save his sister.

Beerappa climbed Akonda, a tall and treacherous hill, in search of the source of the water in Nerri. After much searching, he found nothing. Exhausted, he lay on a rock, listening carefully. Then, he heard a loud sound, echoing everywhere a sound of water crashing down. He realized it was coming from a hidden spot in the valley, with water pouring down from a large rock into the Nerri below.

The sight was daunting. Reaching the water seemed nearly impossible, but Beerappa 's determination surged, driven by the thought of his sister's life being tied to his own. It looked like a small waterfall, with the roots tangled and woven into the water source, forming an intricate network. He knew the *kukkavainta* and *kalasakura* roots were somewhere among them, but finding the right ones felt nearly impossible.

Undeterred, Beerappa saw vines entangled with the roots. He cut the vines, fashioned them into a strong rope, and tied them securely to a tree at the top of the hill. Holding onto the vine rope, he descended into the Nerri, carefully navigating the slippery surfaces covered in moss and plankton. One wrong move and he could have fallen into the depths below.

At the bottom, Beerappa examined the roots, trying to identify the ones he needed. It was hot and humid, with hardly any wind, and the area felt enclosed, as if the sun barely touched the spot. Beerappa, touching everything carefully, finally came across a root that felt like something significant it resembled a small liver, which he thought might be dog roots. When he tried to cut it, the root resisted, confirming it was the *kalasakura* he sought. Beerappa pulled with all his strength, and after a long struggle, he managed to cut the roots.

Climbing back up, Beerappa realized the difficulty of what he had accomplished. Everything seemed on the edge of slipping into the abyss, but he made it back safely. When he looked down into the valley again, he marveled at his achievement before heading back to Mungisur.

Upon his return, Beerappa presented the water soaked roots of Donakonda to Lord Bhagwanthappa.

Nagasheshu, watching Beerappa in awe, bowed deeply, saying, "I have never seen anyone like you in my entire life. I am forever indebted to you."

Beerappa,having fulfilled his promise, took his elder sister, along with the sheep and the horse given to him, and bowed to Lord Bhagwanthappa before leaving the village.

As they traveled, Beerappa and Mayamma continued to graze their sheep, making their way to the Kanuganoor forest. In this forest, several people lived in tents, including a man named Kustikallappa, who was notorious for his strength and arrogance. Kustikallappa, however, was not satisfied with just his physical power. He began eyeing Beerappa 's sister, Mayamma, with ill intentions.

One day, while Beerappa was away gathering leaves for the lambs, Kustikallappa saw Mayamma alone with Rappa. Seizing the opportunity, he attempted to force himself on her, but Mayamma fiercely resisted. Just then, Beerappa returned, scythe in hand. Seeing what was happening, Beerappa swung the back of the scythe, striking

Kallappa hard on the back. The blow was strong enough to leave a deep wound.

Soon, the people of Gudem gathered, surrounding both Beerappa and Kustikallappa, trying to defuse the situation. But Kallappa cried out in pain, and Mayamma, shaken, was afraid. Beerappa,seeing the trouble, said to his sister, "Let's leave this place. We can't live among people like this, with these constant fights."

But Mayamma, uncertain, replied, "Where can we go, brother? We must learn to live among evil people."

Beerappa,resolute, said, "Don't be afraid, Akka. I will deal with him in the right way."

Not long after, the time for the Kanuganoor Peddaparasa festival arrived. It was a grand celebration, marked by wrestling competitions, where the strongest men would compete. This time, however, no one was willing to challenge Kustikallappa. His strength and reputation had made him invincible in the eyes of many. Seeing this, the villagers approached Beerappa and asked him to face Kustikallappa in the wrestling competition.

Beerappa initially refused, wanting to avoid unnecessary conflict. But Kallappa himself approached Beerappa and taunted him, saying, "If you defeat me in wrestling, I will give you my entire herd of sheep and leave this place forever."

Beerappa,seeing an opportunity to end the trouble once and for all, accepted the challenge. It was time for him to show that true strength was not just about brute force but about protecting the ones you love and standing up to those who seek to harm others.

Kustikallappa, desperate to avoid further conflict, told Beerappa,"If you defeat me, I'll give you all my sheep, leave your sister alone, and disappear from this area forever."

The people of Kanuganoor, tired of Kallappa's presence, encouraged Beerappa to accept the challenge. After much persuasion, Beerappa agreed.

The next day, the wrestling competition was arranged. A circle was drawn on the ground for the fight, marked with red powder. People from the village gathered around to watch. A gentleman was present to ensure fair play, ready to punish any violations of the rules. He first explained the wrestling rules to both Beerappa and Kallappa, and the match began.

It felt like two towering hills were colliding as the two men grappled, their strength shaking the ground like rams locking horns. Beerappa quickly gained the upper hand, slipping his foot between Kallappa's legs and flipping him to the ground by his neck. Kallappa, disoriented, struggled to get back up, but Beerappa wasn't finished. He threw Kallappa down again, but Kallappa, though beaten, managed to get a hold of Beerappa and attempted to throw him too. Both men fought fiercely, but Beerappa grabbed Kallappa by the shoulders, turned him around, and lifted him completely off the ground, slamming him down with great force.

As Kallappa hit the ground, the gentleman overseeing the match declared Beerappa the victor. Kallappa, his back shaking with pain and exhaustion, accepted his defeat. As promised, he handed over all his sheep to Beerappa and left the village, never to return.

Beerappa and his sister Mayamma stayed in Kanuganoor, taking over Kallappa's flock of sheep. The villagers were grateful, and Beerappa 's reputation grew. He and Mayamma continued to graze the sheep, living peacefully.

In Kanuganoor, there was a custom of cooking lamb on large rocks. After cooking a lamb, everyone would place the meat on the rock and eat it together. However, despite cooking several lambs, not everyone would get enough food. They would end up cooking more lambs, slaughtering hundreds of sheep without ever fully satisfying the village's hunger.

Mallappa, the leader of the largest shepherd group in Kanuganoor, suggested a new system. "Let's cook ten sheep at a time and serve them. We'll put the cooked meat on the rock and share it equally. That way, we won't have to keep slaughtering all our sheep in vain," he said.

The villagers agreed to try Malappa's method. They slaughtered ten sheep, brought firewood, and cooked the meat together. When the food was served, everyone was able to eat, and the system worked. Malappa's wisdom impressed Beerappa,and seeing his trustworthiness, Beerappa arranged for his sister Mayamma to marry Malappa.

With sheep from both Kallappa and Malappa's herds, Beerappa and Mayamma left Kanuganoor and moved to Kadugiri, where they continued to shear sheep and tend to their flock.

In Kadugiri, there was a notorious problem with wild boars, and the people often spoke of how dangerous the animals were. One day, a wild boar appeared among the sheep, and Boranna, a local shepherd, saw it. He turned to Beerappa and said, "That boar is as good as dead if I see it again."

Beerappa, confident in his abilities, replied, "Let's see who can kill it first." As the boar ran, both Beerappa and Boranna gave chase. Beerappa caught the boar by its hind legs, swung it around, and slammed it to the ground, killing it instantly. Boranna, stunned by Beerappa 's strength, watched in awe. After learning about Beerappa 's defeat of Kallappa in Kanuganoor, Boranna developed great respect for him, and the two became close friends. Together, they tended to their sheep, working side by side.

A few months later, Boranna came to Beerappa with a message. "Mayamma has asked you to come home. She wants to give you turmeric and saffron."

When Boranna delivered Mayamma's message, Beerappa said, "Tell her I won't come. If Ayyappa has sent you to call me and I don't come, then she'll understand how much I've grown. Pass on this message to Ayyappa."

Boranna returned to Mayamma with Beerappa 's words. She was surprised but also proud of her brother's resolve. However, Beerappa, after some reflection, decided to visit his sister in person, and he said, "Alright, I'll go myself this time."

When Beerappa arrived at his sister Mayamma's home, she warmly invited him inside, but Beerappa refused, standing firmly at the door.

"Come inside," she insisted.

"I will not," Beerappa replied.

Mayamma, determined, brought him inside by force, saying, "Come in, brother. Sit down."

"I will not sit," he repeated, his tone stern.

Mayamma, frustrated, said, "You wouldn't come when I sent a man to fetch you. Why? Are sheep more important than family now?"

Beerappa,still standing, replied, "I didn't come because I was busy tending to the sheep.

Trying to ease the tension, Mayamma prepared cheese for her younger brother, but Beerappa refused to eat it.

"I will not eat," he said.

Mayamma, sensing his frustration, asked gently, "What do you want then? I can make you something else."

"I want cheese made from tiger nuts," Beerappa answered, his adventurous spirit still strong.

Mayamma, slightly exasperated, said, "You always seek adventure, brother. Why not eat what's available? Sometimes it's enough just to eat what's before you."

Relenting a bit, Beerappa ate the cheese, and Mayamma then asked him to take her and her husband to Kadugiri, as it wasn't good for her to stay there any longer.

Boranna, the family's trusted helper, prepared everything Mayamma had requested, including turmeric and saffron, and the family headed back to Kadugiri. However, Beerappa 's sternness left Mayamma feeling upset by her younger brother's demeanor. Still, she blessed him, hoping for his wellbeing.

As time passed, it seemed Mayamma's blessings worked wonders. All the sheep in Beerappa 's herd began giving birth to twins, and his flock grew exponentially, bringing him more wealth and prosperity.

Boranna, who had been helping Beerappa,soon decided to take a journey of his own and asked Beerappa to take care of the sheep while he was away. Meanwhile, Beerappa decided to visit his sister again.

Mayamma was overjoyed to see her younger brother again. She welcomed him warmly, offering him food and asking various questions about his wellbeing and the sheep. "Sister, everything is fine," Beerappa assured her. "Your blessings have kept me well. But now, I have another task. I need to bring our mother to live with us, to resolve the anger she has toward me, and to honor our father's memory."

Mayamma, sensing Beerappa 's growing responsibilities, tried to guide him. "You don't need to kill anyone, brother. The person who insulted you, let him be. Show him who you are through your actions, not through violence. Instead, you should marry his daughter, and I will be there to perform aarti for you."

But Beerappa firmly rejected the idea. "I do not want to marry, sister. My mission is to help those in need, to protect those in danger, and to ensure justice is done. Marriage will only hinder my ambitions."

Mayamma, knowing the danger of Beerappa 's uncle Bettappa's plans, tried to convince him. "Brother, your uncle's desire is to see you fail. He wants to see you destroyed. You don't need to kill him or his plans; you must prove yourself by succeeding in life. Marry his daughter and bring her here, and all will be set right." Reluctantly, Beerappa agreed to consider his sister's words and set off for Meshanadu, where Bettappa lived.

At the same time, Beerappa 's childhood friend Malinga, who couldn't bear the thought of being left behind, set out through the forest in search of Beerappa . Without telling his family, Malinga journeyed through the wild, making small noises to scare away any wild animals lurking in the shadows.

Malinga sustained himself by eating wild fruits he found along the way, but after days of walking, he became exhausted. He lay down under a tree to rest, only to wake up with a shock a snake was coiled around his waist. Terrified, Malinga sprang up, unsure of what to do next. As Malinga sat up in the tree, the rain poured relentlessly. He couldn't tell if it was day or night; it was just rain, pouring without end. Exhausted and scared, he clung to the branches, unable to climb down. Meanwhile, Beerappa,who had stopped his journey due to the rain, noticed someone sitting high in a tree in the forest. When the rain slowed, Beerappa ventured down from the hill, calling out in his usual manner, making a bubbling sound. To his surprise, Malinga, hearing the sound, responded from the tree.

Beerappa hurried to the tree and was shocked to see his childhood friend. "Malinga! What are you doing here?" he asked in surprise.

Malinga slowly climbed down from the tree, his limbs stiff from being perched there for so long. He explained everything how he had been wrapped by a snake, nearly drowned in the flood, and had taken refuge in the tree from the terrible rain.

Beerappa listened and then asked, "But why did you come all the way out here?"

Malinga, still panting from the experience, replied, "I came looking for you. I was worried."

Beerappa,with serious s said, "I'm in a difficult situation right now. Just like how you barely escaped the flood, I'm caught in a deep struggle too."

Malinga looked at him, concerned. "What's happening, Beerappa ?"

Beerappa sighed. "I found out from my sister that I'm not Lingaya's son. I've been traveling to Chandragiri to find my real mother."

Malinga, ever loyal, said, "Let's go together and meet her."

But Beerappa shook his head. "No, Malinga. I don't want you to suffer because of me. I remember when my mother scolded you and me as children. I don't want to bring you more trouble. Please, go back to your home or greet my sister and leave."

But Malinga refused to be. "I came all this way for you, and I won't go back alone."

Beerappa,seeing Malinga's determination, said, "There is a place far from here called Bhaveli. In a well near Bhaveli, there are many flowers. I was asked to collect those flowers to worship my Lord Pashupati. But it's a dangerous place."

Malinga, not backing down, said, "I'll get them for you."

Beerappa hesitated. "No, there's a snake in that well, one that doesn't harm anyone but guards the water and the flowers. It has a long history."

Curious, Malinga asked, "What's the story behind it?"

Beerappa began to recount the tale. "Long ago, when people camped with their cattle near Bhaveli, demons came and killed everyone in the camp, stealing their cattle and sheep. Everyone in the camp fled for their lives. Among the survivors were women named Vokayamma and Audayamma. They lived in constant fear of the demons. One day, Vokayamma, unable to bear the torment, ran away from the others and threw herself into the well. Since then, it's believed that her spirit guards the well, appearing in the form of a snake. No one dares go down into that well, as they say her spirit roams there, still seeking justice."

Beerappa,seeing the troubled look on Malinga's face, added, "It's not just the snake you need to worry about. The well is said to be cursed. Those who try to enter are haunted by her spirit."

Malinga, thinking about the story, wondered if there was more to it. "Those full eyes... they remind me of something my mother used to tell me when I was young. What if Vokayamma is someone from my past, or even yours?" He began to think more deeply, connecting the story with his own memories.

As Beerappa watched Malinga in deep thought, he reflected too. "Maybe this is more than just a story to frighten people. Perhaps there's a deeper meaning to it all."

For a moment, they both sat in silence, unsure of what to do next. The weight of the past, present, and future hung heavy in the air, as they pondered the journey ahead.

Malinga, undeterred by the danger and haunted by the uncertainty, said, "No matter what, I will go with you and fetch whatever is needed."

He was filled with a sense of loyalty and duty, knowing deep down that no matter what Beerappa said, he couldn't let his friend go alone. They both decided to venture together on the perilous journey.

Meanwhile, Mayamma, Beerappa 's elder sister, was heartbroken since her brother had left. She felt as though her life had drained away. She could hardly eat, lost in her thoughts and worries about Beerappa . Where could he be? What could have happened to him? These questions haunted her day and night. Every few days, she would wake up from a restless sleep, disturbed by nightmares.

Beerappa, disguised to avoid suspicion, finally reached Chandragiri. He learned about Munjamma's house from the children tending sheep in the area.

"If you feed our sheep all day, we will show you where Munjamma's house is," the children said.

Beerappa agreed and spent the entire day watching over their sheep. As evening approached, the children kept their promise and led Beerappa to Munjamma's house.

Munjamma, Bettappa's daughter, regularly brought flowers to Kannikamakka. Beerappa approached her and introduced himself in disguise.

"I will give you a hundred sheep if you take me to Kannikamakka," Beerappa offered.

Munjamma hesitated, knowing her father's cruelty. "My father is a very wicked man. If Ayyappa finds out, he will kill me. He even tried to kill you in your mother's womb. How can I go against such a man who murdered his own brother in law?"

Beerappa reassured her, "You won't be harmed. I will protect you. Just help me this once."

But Munjamma refused. "No, I cannot do it. The danger is too great. I can't risk it."

Seeing her fear, Beerappa pleaded with her. "Let me stay in your home, just for a short while. No one will know."

Reluctantly, Munjamma agreed, and Beerappa took shelter in her home. While Munjamma busied herself with her work, preparing a flower garland for Kannikamakka, Beerappa offered to help. "You do your other tasks, I will finish making the garland," Beerappa said.

Munjamma, hesitant but tired, agreed. "Fine, but please don't ruin it. This garland must be perfect."

As Beerappa worked on the garland, he unknowingly tied his ring into it, making the garland heavier. When Munjamma saw the finished garland, she was astonished. "This isn't just any garland! You must be someone extraordinary to make such a beautiful creation so effortlessly. You're no ordinary person."

The next day, Munjamma brought the garland to Kannikamakka as usual. When Kannikamakka saw the garland, she was amazed by its beauty and precision. "Who made this garland?" she asked. "This is not like any other garland I've seen."

Munjamma, nervous, replied, "My little sister tied it yesterday at our home."

As Kannikamakka admired the garland, the ring that Beerappa had accidentally woven into it fell to the ground. Surprised, Kannikamakka asked, "Who created this garland so beautifully, and whose ring is this?"

Munjamma, confused, said, "I don't know about the ring, but my younger sister made the garland."

Kannikamakka, intrigued, says, "Bring that girl to me tomorrow. I must meet her."

Munjamma, trying to avoid suspicion, said, "She's very shy and doesn't like going anywhere."

Kannikamakka smiled and insisted, "If she won't come, bring her all the gifts I have prepared for her."

Munjamma returned home and told Beerappa everything that had happened. Early the next morning, Beerappa disguised himself again, this time wearing the garland and with the gifts given by Kannikamakka. He prepared to meet her.

When they finally met, Beerappa and Munjamma exchanged knowing looks. Beerappa embraced Munjamma with affection, but something in the air felt off. Kannikamakka began to suspect that something was amiss. She observed Beerappa carefully, sensing that he was not who he appeared to be. Her intuition told her that this might be an impersonation.

Kannikamakka tried to confirm her suspicions by attempting to touch Beerappa, thinking the disguise would be revealed. But Beerappa, fully aware of the danger, skillfully avoided her attempts, ensuring that his disguise remained intact. He knew that any slip could lead to disaster, so he stayed vigilant, waiting for the right moment to reveal his true identity.

The next day, Beerappa disguised himself as a glassblower and went to the fort where Kannikamavva lived. Upon seeing him, Kannikamavva, intrigued, asked her mother to summon Gajulammeva to remove her glass ornaments. At the time, Bettappa was not home, and things seemed calm.

Following her daughter's request, Kannikamavva's mother called for Gajulammeva, and the glass ornaments were carefully removed. While this process took time, Beerappa, feeling a bit stiff from standing, spread his legs to stretch. At that moment, Kannikamavva noticed something peculiar the Shankhangurtu (conch shaped) birthmark on Beerappa 's leg.

Impressed by how skillfully he handled the glass ornaments, Kannikamavva gifted Beerappa something as a token of gratitude. Guttakka, her mother, later mentioned the event to Bettappa when he returned home.

Bettappa, growing suspicious, asked her, "Tell me exactly what happened. What did this man look like?"

Guttakka described the man's appearance: "He had a bald head, a black mustache, and a dark body, and he seemed to move with ease."

Bettappa pressed further, "Did you notice anything else?"

"When he stretched his leg, I saw a cone shaped mole," Guttakka replied.

Hearing this, Bettappa immediately understood who had visited. "That's not just anyone that's Beerappa, your father's enemy," Bettappa warned. He immediately ordered strict security around the area, insisting that no one was to enter the fort. He knew someone had been wandering around, and his suspicions about Beerappa 's presence grew stronger.

Unbeknownst to Bettappa, Beerappa had cleverly stayed in Guttakka's house under the old woman's nose. Meanwhile, Kannikamavva's thoughts were consumed by the man she had met.

That very night, after everyone had fallen asleep, Kannikamavva made her way to Munjamma's house. She couldn't shake the image of the mysterious man and had to find out more. When she arrived, she inquired about her "brother in law" with a sense of desperation.

Munjamma, knowing the truth, tried to console her. But Kannikamavva insisted, "My brother in law is here, and I am indebted to you for reuniting me with him. He will take me from here no matter what."

Beerappa, sensing the gravity of the situation, gently said, "No, Kannikamavva, I am not here for marriage. I am searching for my mother."

But Kannikamavva couldn't hold back her emotions. "I cannot leave you, Beerappa . The people in my village believe I was born for you. Because of you, the marriage that was supposed to happen for me in Mavur has been canceled. People are calling me mad. Please, take me away from here."

Munjamma, deeply moved, added, "This is a blood relation, Nayana, not something to be easily escaped. You must take this girl and marry her."

Realizing there was no way to turn back, Beerappa agreed. That very night, he took Kannikamavva with him and rode directly on horseback to seek the blessings of his elder sister.

As they arrived, Beerappa 's elder sister and others rushed to greet them. Everyone was filled with joy upon seeing Beerappa,and they marveled at the beauty of Kannikamavva. "Amma's niece has brought a girl as radiant as gold! Look how beautiful she is, like a tree and vine intertwined," they exclaimed.

Beerappas older sister came out from inside the house, overjoyed to see her younger brother standing there with happiness on his face. But tears welled up in her eyes as she spoke, "I never thought I'd live to see your wedding day, and now that I have, my heart is full."

Meanwhile, their mother, who had been asleep, suddenly woke up, tears rolling down her cheeks. She sat up, confused, wondering if she had just had a vivid dream. She drank some water and lay down again, reflecting on how she hadn't had a peaceful night's sleep in four years. "Could it really have been a dream?" she thought. "Or has something truly happened to my younger brother?"

As she sat in her bed, deep in thought, she heard a familiar sound a bubbling sound, echoing through the air. She listened closely, recognizing it as Beerappa 's unique call. Filled with hope, she followed the sound, and as she ventured out, she met Adivanna, who had been following the same bubbling sound from the other side.

Both of them met along the path, sitting under a tree for a while, exchanging stories and catching up. When Adivanna asked, Beerappa introduced himself, sharing his journey and revealing the incredible story of everything that had happened up until that moment. They both felt a sense of fate guiding them, as though the bubbling sounds and the events of the night were signs that something great was yet to come.

Beerappa, still piecing everything together, asked Adivanna, "Are you familiar with all of this? Do you know the details of my past?"

Adivanna smiled knowingly. "I know every tree in this forest, every story connected to them. I've walked this land for a long time."

Curious, Adivanna asked, "Where do you come from?"

Beerappa replied, "We are from Kalgiri."

Adivanna's eyes widened with recognition. "There's no one in Kalgiri I don't know, no one who hasn't seen me. Do you know Lingaya?"

Beerappa nodded. "Yes, I'm his son."

Adivanna smiled again. "Ah, Lingaya, yes. But he has no children of his own. Both children he raised were found after being abandoned in the bushes. In fact, I gave him one of those children, knowing he was childless."

Beerappas heart raced, realizing he had met the man who saved him as a child. "You… you're the one who gave me to Lingaya?"

Adivanna nodded. "Yes, you were left hanging from a tree with ropes, and I searched everywhere, finding no one to claim you. Later, I found out you were Suramma's son. I didn't tell Suramma about it all these years, knowing your uncle was plotting to kill you."

At the mention of his mother, Beerappas eyes welled up with emotion. "Where are my mother and father now? I need to see them."

Adivanna sighed deeply. "Manikasura and Mallasura, the house robbers, called your father and forced him into their schemes. Your father in law made sure their plan was executed perfectly. They tried to blame Lingaiah for the crimes, to ruin his name."

He continued, "Your mother,  along with your aunt Muddamma, have been worshiping the Shivalinga near the animal sanctuary. They've been through a lot."

Hearing this, Beerappa 's anger boiled over. "So it's my uncle who is behind all the suffering my family has endured?"

Adivanna nodded solemnly. Beerappa clenched his fists, furious at his uncle's treachery.

"Will you come with me to the cattle farm?" Beerappa asked Adivanna.

"Of course," Adivanna replied. "I owe your father Barama for the journey we shared, and I will stand with you now."

Together, Beerappa,Adivanna, and Malinga set out for the animal sanctuary. As they arrived, they saw that all the roofs of the temple had been removed, leaving the sanctuary exposed to the elements.

Near the temple, Beerappa spotted Suramma working beneath a tree, her frail body moving slowly as she cared for Pantumusali, who lay nearby, weak and disfigured. The sight broke Beerappa 's heart his mother, in such a weakened state, tending to another with such devotion.

Muddamma's body was swollen, and she looked nauseous, while Suramma tirelessly cared for her. Beerappa,overcome with emotion, approached them slowly. As Suramma looked up, she didn't immediately recognize her grown son. There was a glow in her tired eyes, and she held her hands together tightly, as if praying for the survival of her long lost child.

She glanced from Beerappa to Adivanna, and in that moment, Adivanna's eyes conveyed the truth. Suramma's face softened, her gaze full of love and confusion. She stared at Beerappa,unsure but hopeful. Could this be her son, the one she had lost so many years ago?

Tears welled up in Beerappa 's eyes as he knelt before her. "What are you thinking, Amma? Do you wonder who stands before you? It is your son, Veerudamma. I will now stand against all the troubles that have haunted you."

Suramma's hands trembled as she reached out to touch her son's face, recognizing the truth in his words. Tears streamed down her cheeks, and she pulled him close, embracing him with the love and relief she had longed for all these years.

Beerappa 's journey had finally brought him home, but the battles ahead were far from over. Yet, in this moment, he had found his mother, and that was the strength he needed to face whatever came next.

Suramma, still struggling to comprehend the reality before her, stared again at Beerappa 's face. Her eyes fell on the conch shaped mole that marked his leg, and in that instant, it was as if the whole earth shook with the realization. Her lips quivered, her legs trembled, and her eyes, once filled with sorrow, now brimmed with tears of overwhelming joy. It was as if the universe itself was moved by this long awaited reunion, with the earth trembling in harmony with the emotions flooding their hearts.

Tears, full of love and pride, began flowing from Suramma's eyes like a river washing over her son's feet, as if in worship. Even the surroundings, so silent and motionless before, seemed to hum with life, moved by the profound moment of a mother and son finally reunited.

Adivanna, witnessing this sacred scene, couldn't help but wipe away his own tears. The reunion was so powerful that even the most hardened hearts would have melted at the sight. Kannathallidi, overwhelmed with pride, let her own tears flow, not just for the reunion but for the honor of seeing her hero son stand before her, stronger than ever. The love between mother and son filled the air, and even the old serpents around them were enchanted, swaying in the air as if in a dance, captivated by the scent of wild jasmine carried by the breeze.

Words were unnecessary in that moment. Their hearts spoke in silence, their emotions sharing what their mouths could not. The love they had for each other passed between them like an unspoken language, filling the space with a warmth that transcended all the pain of the past.

Finally, Adivanna broke the silence and asked Suramma, "Who did this to the temple? Who has left it in such a state?"

Suramma, with a heavy heart, replied, "The army of Manikasuras and Mallasuras have been staying in this temple. They came here, stealing the silver elephants and kasalas."

Beerappa 's fury erupted. Grabbing his ax, he was ready to seek justice, his heart blazing with the fire of righteous anger.

But Suramma quickly grabbed his arm, her voice trembling with fear. "No, Beerappa,don't go after them. They will kill you."

Adivanna, calm yet firm, reassured her. "Amma, your son is no ordinary man. He has made the impossible possible before, and these demons cannot harm him."

Suramma, still afraid, said, "But Bettappa supports them. They have supernatural powers, and he stands with them."

Beerappa,his face determined, asked, "Supernatural powers? What powers do they have?"

Suramma explained, "Manikasura and Mallasura once disturbed the penance of ancient sages on Manichulaparvatam. They mocked the sages and committed many wrongs. In a fit of anger, one of the sages struck Manikasura's cheek, cursing them to die like dogs, worse than dogs. But those demons didn't stop. After killing the sages and the villagers, they swore that the curse would never touch them. They went to Lord Shiva, seeking a way to escape the curse."

Beerappa,shocked, asked, "Lord Shiva appeared to such demons?"

Suramma nodded. "Yes, it is said that they performed such powerful penance that even Shiva could not ignore them."

Beerappa pressed on, "And what did they ask for?"

Suramma sighed, continuing the story. "They asked Lord Shiva to make them invincible in battle. They wanted a boon that no matter who they fought in the world, they would not die. They also asked that if a drop of their blood touched the ground, a thousand more of them would rise from that single drop. Lord Shiva, though hesitant, granted their wish. He told them, 'As you have asked, so it shall be.'"

"With that boon," Suramma continued, "they have terrorized the shepherds and the villagers. No one has dared stand against them because of their power. They are untouchable, and their actions know no bounds. Even with the curse upon them, their evil has grown, and they continue to bring misery to everyone around them."

The gravity of the situation hit Beerappa hard. These were not ordinary enemies. They were beings who had been blessed with a deadly gift, one that made them nearly impossible to defeat. But Beerappa was not one to back down from a challenge, no matter how powerful the adversary.

"They may have their powers," Beerappa said, his voice steady, "but I have something stronger my love for my family, my people, and my purpose. I will not let them continue their reign of terror. They will face justice."

Suramma, though still fearful for her son's safety, saw the unwavering determination in Beerappa 's eyes. She knew that he would not rest until the Manikasuras and Mallasuras were stopped.

Adivanna placed a hand on Beerappa 's shoulder, nodding in agreement. "You have the strength, Beerappa,and now it's time to use it. We will face them together."

Suramma, with deep insight, explained to Beerappa that the strength of Manikasura and Mallasura was tied to the beads they wore. "Their power," she said, "comes from those beads. But don't be disheartened. All they have is stolen through treachery and evil deeds. If Lord Shiva gave them this power for their penance, imagine how much more power He can give to good devotees like us."

She reassured Beerappa,"Don't be afraid, my son. You have the strength and the righteousness to face them. I believe in you."

With a newfound determination, Beerappa, along with Adivanna, made his way back to Kalgiri. As they entered the village, a joyful Lingaya rushed out of the tent, overjoyed to see Beerappa again.

"Oh, where have you been all these years? Where is your sister? What happened to both of you?" he asked eagerly, his face full of relief and hope.

Beerappa told him everything that had happened the trials they faced, the journey he had undertaken to find his mother, and his encounters with the supernatural powers of Manikasura and Mallasura.

Then, Beerappa visited Malinga's mother, Umadevi. The moment she saw her son, her heart filled with joy, and she seemed to come back to life.

"Oh, my son, when did you return? Where have you been all these years?" she wept, holding onto Malinga. "Was it fair to leave without saying a word to your mother, who was living her hopes on you?"

Malinga comforted his mother, saying, "Amma, I haven't been far. You've always been in my heart. Even when I drank water, I remembered you. Even when I slept under trees, it felt like sleeping in your arms."

He then added, "I went looking for Beerappa,and he found me too. Now that Beerappa is with me, I will be fine. If Beerappa is with me, I will eat and live. If he's not, I won't."

Beerappa chimed in, "I am not ready for marriage yet, Amma. My heart and soul are devoted to helping others. Don't push Malinga into this he has his own path."

But Umadevi, with a mother's wisdom, said, "Beerappa, you are a hero, yes, but there are some things even heroes cannot avoid. Malinga is right to stay by your side. He looks up to you, and that's why he won't leave you."

Amma insisted, "I will do marriage for you,but malinga said that he will marry after we return victorious from Managudem."

At that moment, Malinga's face changed as Beerappa told him the truth about his real parents Barama and Suramma. With reverence, Malinga bowed before his mother and departed, following

Beerappa 's lead. His mother blessed him through her tears, calling for divine protection over her son.

With a sense of purpose, Beerappa prepared an army of one hundred dogs with the help of Lingaya, and they set off to confront Manikasura and Mallasura.

As they marched through the forest, Beerappa and Adivanna heard a familiar sound the sound of bubbling, echoing through the trees. The dogs accompanying them barked in response, their instincts sharpened.

Adivanna, sensing danger, whispered, "Manikasura and Mallasura are nearby. The sound gives them away."

Beerappa 's anger boiled within him as he recalled the fact that these demons had killed his father. Then, they heard the bleating of sheep nearby.

Adivanna confirmed, "It must be them. Today, on Aries day, they steal sheep and cattle from around Chandragiri and terrorize the shepherds."

Without hesitation, Beerappa sped forward like the wind, determined to face the demons. As he arrived, he saw Manikasura and Mallasura sitting under a tree, roasting sheep and eating, as if they were preparing for war.

Their thirty dogs were engaged in a fierce fight with the dogs that Beerappa had brought with him. The scene resembled a battleground, with the two sides locked in combat.

Beerappa,filled with righteous fury, immediately signaled to Malinga, Adivanna, and Lingaya to stay by his side as they approached the demons. His first priority was to save the sheep and protect the villagers from further terror.

While Manikasura and Mallasura continued to eat, oblivious to the brewing storm, Beerappa strategized. He knew that to defeat these supernatural beings, he needed more than brute strength he needed to outsmart them.

As Beerappa readied himself for the fight of his life, he was determined not only to avenge his father's death but also to put an end to the reign of terror that Manikasura and Mallasura had inflicted on the land. He tightened his grip on his axe, his eyes fixed on the demons, knowing that the time for justice had come.

Manikasura, seething with rage, charged toward Beerappa, determined to crush the man who dared to stand against him. But Beerappa was ready. With swift precision, he thrust his barji (spear) deep into Manikasura's throat. Blood spurted from the wound, and before it could touch the ground, the dogs leapt forward, licking it away, ensuring that no more demons could rise from the blood.

Mallasura and his army, witnessing their leader fall, panicked. The dogs chased them through the forest, bringing down the fleeing demons one by one. They tore at Mallasura's throat, draining his blood before it could spill. The demons, who once terrorized the land, were no more. Beerappa stood tall, victorious, watching as the fires burned their bodies to ash.

The news of Beerappa 's triumph spread like wildfire. From Meshanadu to Chandragiri and Kalgiri, people whispered the tale of the hero who had slain the terrifying demons. Bettappa, upon hearing the news, was stricken with fear. "If Beerappa has killed Manikasura and Mallasura, what chance do I have?" he thought.

Meanwhile, Beerappa,along with Adivanna and Lingayya, made their way to the Shiva temple, where his mother, Suramma, was waiting. Together, they went to Meshanadu, to Rappadal, and Beerappa prepared himself for the final confrontation with his treacherous uncle, Bettappa.

Bettappa, realizing his defeat was near, tried to flee. But Suramma stood firm, blocking his path. "Uncle," she said, " you were like a mother to me. Yet you are the one who created all these conspiracies and brought such hardship upon us."

"You are my blood, my nephew," Beerappa said, stepping forward. "A nephew's bond is more sacred than even a child's. You tried to sever this bond, but now I hold your life in my hands. I won't kill you, but you are already dead to me. You tried to flee, and in my eyes, that makes you as good as gone."

Kannikamavva, watching silently, realized that the man she had waited for all these years had finally come. Beerappa,stoic and calm, turned to the gathered villagers. According to their custom, someone who had committed grave sins had to carry untied clothes on their head as a mark of shame. But before that could happen, the villagers began calling for Bettappa's daughter to be married to Beerappa .

Following tradition, Beerappa whispered into the ear of a ram from the flock. The ram was then released, and it ran straight to Suramma's house, stopping at the entrance. The villagers erupted with joy, taking this as a sign of approval from the gods.

Turning back to Bettappa, Beerappa said, "You thought that by my birth, your death was assured, didn't you? You sacrificed my entire family out of fear, but you're still standing here. Life and death aren't determined by one person's birth, Uncle. If that were the case, the world wouldn't see so many births. You listened to someone who told you that I was destined to kill you. But where is that person now? In my hands, defeated. I didn't even know my mother's voice when I was born, and only now do I recognize her when she stands in front of me. Your ignorance is the root of all this suffering."

Bettappa and Guttakka, overcome with shame, could not raise their heads. They had lost everything.

Kannikamavva slowly approached Beerappa,her eyes filled with love and relief. Meanwhile, Muddamma, full of pride for her grandson, called out in joy. Beerappa led his mother, Suramma, to the spot where his father had died and performed the rites, burying a Nitrai (sacred staff) there in his honor, offering it as a tribute to the fallen.

Before leaving, Beerappa entrusted Adivanna with the task of taking good care of Lingaya, ensuring the village would remain protected. Then, with his mother Suramma and his sister in law Kannikamavva by his side, he left, embarking on the next chapter of their lives.

As they reached their destination, Beerappa knelt before his mother and Kannikamavva, both of whom were not widowed but now free from the shackles of their tragic past. Together, they moved forward, their hearts filled with peace, ready to embrace the new life that awaited them.

Beerappa,now victorious, prepared for the next step in his life with his close companions by his side. He took Malinga along, saying they must now arrange for his marriage. The desire to inspire and create more heroes like Beerappa was strong. *"Shivane Nammaneyadyavaru Bandarabannire, Swami Nammaneyadyavaru Bandarabannire"* chants of devotion filled the air as they prepared to celebrate.

Vosikeri, deeply moved, reflected on the extensive research he had done over the past eight months. He thought about the depth of Beerappa 's story and how much more there was to write. "If I write more, this history will only expand further," he thought. But for now, he decided, this part of Beerappa 's history was enough. The project was complete, but there was still much to uncover. He knew that after receiving the recognition and awards for his research, he would return to dive deeper into the story and present an even more comprehensive account.

Vosikeri felt a sense of pride and accomplishment. This research had taken him months of effort, and Beerappa 's story had become such an essential part of his work. Vosikeri smiled at his friend and asked, "Tell me, Vosikerappa, what do you want for helping me complete this project?"

Vosikerappa humbly replied, "I don't want money, just a printed copy of the book. I did this work for the pride of our community, not for personal gain. Reading Beerappa 's story brought tears to my eyes. There is still so much more history to write, and I know there will be many more books to come. If you print this, it will be more than enough for me."

Vosikeri reassured him, "Tomorrow, I will submit the project. After that, we'll bring it to print."

True to his word, Vosikeri submitted the project the next day. Coincidentally, on the same day, the results of the Civil Servises exams that Gagan, his eldest son, had written three months earlier were announced.

The anticipation had been building for days, and the family gathered in hope. The results came in, and Gagan had been selected! The family was overjoyed, and Vosikerappa couldn't help but feel that Beerappa 's influence had played a role in his son's success.

"Do you see the greatness of our home god?" Vosikerappa said with pride, attributing Gagan's selection to divine intervention.

Nagamma, Gagan's mother, responded wisely, "Lord, I won't deny the effort of our home god. But remember, Gagan has been working hard, preparing even before you started this project. If we do anything with sincerity, the results will come naturally."

She continued, "It's a coincidence that the project submission and Gagan's results came on the same day, but both bring immense happiness. It's common for people to attribute their success to divine intervention, but we must acknowledge that hard work and perseverance are key. Some people may gain wealth without toil, but they miss the satisfaction and lessons that come from real effort. We must remember that we belong to society and are accountable for our actions."

The next morning, Gagan's achievement made headlines in all the leading newspapers. His success in the civil service exams, with the headline "Civils Results: Karuvunela Kantipunjam Gagan," was written in bold capital letters, and the family couldn't have been prouder.

Nagamma's joy knew no bounds. She set aside all her worries and organized a grand party for everyone in their neighborhood. Even those who had never acknowledged them before came to celebrate Gagan's success. Nagamma and Vosikeri, along with their children and relatives, including Nagasheshu, went out for a celebratory dinner at a restaurant.

Nagamma, in her exuberance, encouraged everyone, "Drink as much as you want! Tonight, we celebrate my son's achievement!" She shared Gagan's success with her brothers in law and relatives on a video call, spreading her happiness far and wide.

The joy was infectious, and Vosikeri felt overwhelmed with pride for his son.

The next day, Gagan was scheduled to take his official appointment order in Delhi. The family boarded the first flight from Tirupati, with excitement buzzing around them.

Gagan officially received his appointment as a Collector in Uttar Pradesh. That evening, they were invited to a celebratory dinner at Andhra Bhavan in Delhi. Despite the grand hospitality and luxurious surroundings, Vosikeri couldn't sleep. His mind wandered back to Gondipalli, his humble village. He marveled at how far they had come from the simplicity of their home to the bustling, prestigious halls of Delhi.

"What a journey this has been," Vosikeri thought to himself, still trying to grasp the incredible transformation that had unfolded in his life. He realized that this was only the beginning of the legacy they were building, a legacy shaped by faith, hard work, and a deep sense of purpose.

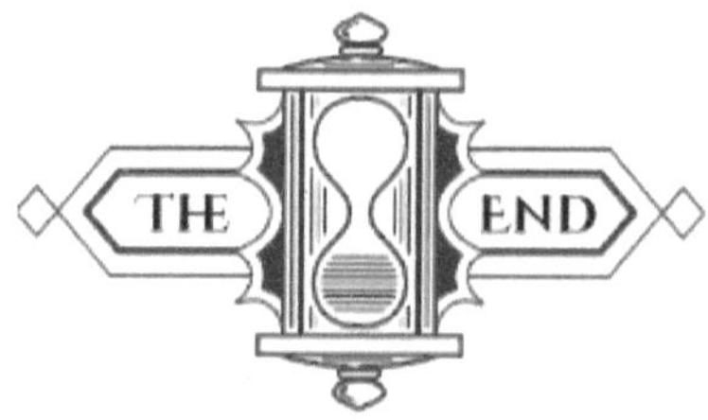

THE
END

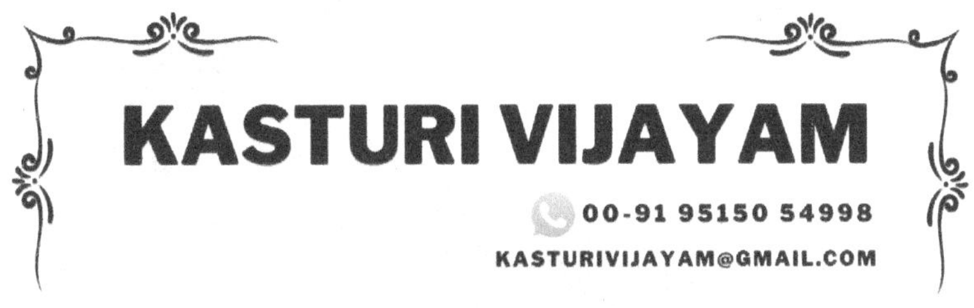


# SUPPORTS

- PUBLISH YOUR BOOK AS YOUR OWN PUBLISHER.

- PAPERBACK & E-BOOK SELF-PUBLISHING

- SUPPORT PRINT ON-DEMAND.

- YOUR PRINTED BOOKS AVAILABLE AROUND THE WORLD.

- EASY TO MANAGE YOUR BOOK'S LOGISTICS AND TRACK YOUR REPORTING.

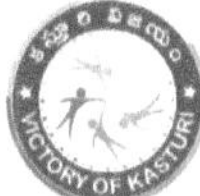